STOCK MARKET INVESTING FOR BEGINNERS

2 books in 1 - The Ultimate Collection to Create Passive Income and Achieve Financial Freedom with Dividend and ETF

BY
HENRY COOPER

© **Copyright 2020 by Henry Cooper All rights reserved.**

This document is geared towards providing exact and reliable information in regards to the topic and issue covered. The publication is sold with the idea that the publisher is not required to render accounting, officially permitted or otherwise qualified services. If advice is necessary, legal or professional, a practiced individual in the profession should be ordered.

From a Declaration of Principles which was accepted and approved equally by a Committee of the American Bar Association and a Committee of Publishers and Associations.

In no way is it legal to reproduce, duplicate, or transmit any part of this document in either electronic means or printed format. Recording of this publication is strictly prohibited, and any storage of this document is not allowed unless with written permission from the publisher. All rights reserved.

The information provided herein is stated to be truthful and consistent, in that any liability, in terms of inattention or otherwise, by any usage or abuse of any policies, processes, or directions contained within is the installments and utter responsibility of the recipient reader. Under no circumstances will any legal responsibility or blame be held against the publisher for any reparation, damages, or monetary loss due to the information herein, either directly or indirectly.

Respective authors own all copyrights not held by the publisher.

The information herein is offered for informational purposes solely and is universal as so. The presentation of the information is without a contract or any type of guarantee assurance.

The trademarks that are used are without any consent, and the publication of the trademark is without permission or backing by the trademark owner. All trademarks and brands within this book are for clarifying purposes only and are owned by the owners themselves, not affiliated with this document.

THANKS YOU

Before you start, I just wanted to say thank you for purchasing my book.

You could have picked from thousands of other books on the same topic but you took a chance and chose this one.

So, a HUGE thanks to you for getting this book.

Now I wanted to ask you for a small favor. Could you please consider posting a review on the platform? Reviews are one of the easiest ways to support the work of independent authors.

This feedback will help me continue to make the type of books that will help you get the results you want.

Follow the link to leave a review or go on your account.

https://www.amazon.com/review/create-review?

Table of Contents

Dividend Investing

Introduction 1

Chapter One: Introduction To Dividend Investing 5

Chapter Two: Dividend Investing For New Investors 14

Chapter Three: Taxation On Dividend Investment 23

Chapter Four: Passive Income 34

Chapter Five: Passive Income And Dividend Investing 62

Chapter Six: Introduction To Financial Freedom 70

Chapter Seven: Dividend Investing For Financial Freedom 86

Chapter Eight: Dividend Stocks For 2020 102

Chapter Nine: Value Of Dividend Growth Investing 109

Chapter Ten: Risks Of Dividend Investing 115

Chapter 11: Top 10 Rookie Mistakes To Avoid 124

Conclusion 129

References 132

Etf Investing

Introduction 139

Chapter One: Understanding Etfs 142

Chapter Two: Why Etfs? 148

Chapter Three: Buying Etfs 160

Chapter Four: Your Portfolio 173

Chapter Five: Let's Talk Trends And Tools 183

Chapter Six: International Investment 202

Chapter Seven: Yummy Sectors 212

Chapter Eight: Gold And Black Gold 220

Chapter Nine: Fixed Income 230

Chapter Ten: Leverage 245

Conclusion 251

References 254

DIVIDEND INVESTING

The Beginner's Guide to Create Passive Income and Achieve Financial Freedom with Stocks

By
Henry Cooper

INTRODUCTION

The Beginners Guide to Create Passive Income and Achieve Financial Freedom with Stocks contains proven steps and strategies on how to invest in dividend stocks and reap the long term benefits to attain financial independence. This invaluable guide to dividend investing will teach you how to generate passive income, identify stocks that yield higher returns and structure your investments for financial security and wellbeing.

Investment in dividend stocks is a less risky and a sensible way to make money grow. Investors with burned riches in recent meltdowns are desperate for risk-free ways to grow their income. This book will help you understand dividend investing and explain how it offers investors a chance to create a steady stream of income.

Buying dividends with higher returns can offer financial security as long as you know which stocks to invest in and are careful to follow the guidelines.

Find a list of the best dividend stocks for 2020 inside!

The major purpose of making dividend investments is to

seek financial safety. As a result, it is important to invest in safe dividends. The dividend coverage ratio is a method that helps determine how much a company earns and how much it pays out in dividends. A company paying less in dividends is eventually a safer choice.

However, don't give yourself a false sense of comfort by accepting a low dividend payout ratio. Ultimately, dividend safety depends on a stable income and cash flow. The more stable the influx of cash is, the higher will be the dividend payout ratio without having to compromise on dividend safety.

The next important step is to focus on high dividend yields. It is important to go for a high dividend yield strategy for a large cash income. A high dividend yield often comes from companies with a slow growth rate. These companies have substantial capital to fund dividend payments.

Another method to maintain a sustainable cash income is to approach the high dividend growth rate strategy. This strategy involves investing in dividend stocks of companies paying lower than the average dividend rate. However, these companies are growing at such a rapid pace that within a decade, the dividend yield will grow significantly alongside profits.

Example

Take, for example, company A, which has a 3.7% dividend yield and an annual dividend growth rate of at least 4% each year. Its current dividend payout ratio is 58%.

Now consider company B with a dividend yield of only

0.90%, but a growth rate of 19% in its dividend payout. Its current dividend payout ratio is 11%.

Most people only trade dividend stocks and do not hold them. If you only buy a dividend stock to get dividend payments and then sell it, you will have to pay the regular tax rate on your dividend income. However, if the stock is held for 60 days or longer, you get the benefit of paying a low dividend tax. Look for qualifying dividend stocks, and try holding them for a longer period to avail the tax benefit.

If you make dividend investments using a margin account instead of a cash account, you will no longer be liable to pay a low dividend tax rate. Here's how:

Investment through a margin account allows your broker to lend your shares to traders who want to sell the stock, hoping to scoop them up later at a lower price. Now these traders, who will have sold the stock without your permission, will be liable to pay you the amount equivalent to the dividend income you would have received had you held the stock.

Since this income is coming from the trader's bank account and is not actually dividend income, it will not qualify for dividend taxation. So, instead of having to pay a low dividend tax rates, you will have to pay regular taxes on your personal income.

The Beginners Guide to Create Passive Income and Achieve Financial Freedom with Stocks offers detailed insight on passive income, thorough instructions on stock investing for novice investors, and steps to dividend investing your way to financial freedom.

Let's begin with a detailed understanding of dividend stocks and how to gear up for investment in one!

CHAPTER ONE

Introduction to Dividend Investing

What Are Dividend Stocks and How Do I Invest in Them?

Dividend Stocks is the term used for those limited companies that have a good track of paying their shareholders a regular share of their current-year profit earned, in the form of dividends. These usually are well-established, successful, and stable firms that keep on distributing dividends consistently each time they make a profit or at the end of their every financial year.

Investing in stocks with a persistent history of paying dividends regularly is one of the best ways to create wealth to obtain long-term benefits from it. As mentioned before, the dividend paid on stock purchase is the proportionate distribution of the share of profit left with the firm after the division of deduction of interest and tax. However, the firms don't need to pay dividends each time they incur profit, and they may decide to reinvest or retain the profit. But you might not find this case when talking about the dividend stocks.

Dividend Stocks share a portion of their company's earning with their investors regularly. A regular basis can be defined as the policy of the firm, whether it decides to distribute twice a year, once in a year, or at the end of each quarter.

Most US-based firms that have declared dividend stocks pay their investors a specific proportionate amount quarterly and those that make their way to the top receive an increment over time. After this, they have to make their choice whether they will reinvest the dividend or prioritize the withdrawal.

Those who are planning to invest in dividend stocks should know that these are likely to be more stable than growth stocks; therefore, they have the potential capability of diversifying your overall investment portfolio and reducing the risk involved.

How can I invest in dividend stocks?

If you are finding an investment on which you can rely on and can receive a regular income, then dividend stocks might be the most suitable option to consider. And just to let you know that investing in dividend stocks is as easy as buying an ETF through an investment account.

How to Buy Dividend Stocks

Many people are in search of good ways of investment that can give them a satisfactory and a regular return but don't know where and how to make a start. So for those, this chapter is going to be full of details and will allow them to learn about the few initial steps they need to follow before investing their life savings.

1. Decide through which form you want to invest in stocks

There is more than one approach that you might come across when deciding how to invest. This depends on you and how well you are aware of the process of buying and selling stocks.

If you have enough knowledge about the whole procedure and are good with the know-how of this system of the stock exchange and how it works, then you might continue with the approach of do-It-yourself. In this, you will decide on which firm you would like to invest in and how much investment will be sufficient to start with. After this, you only need a brokerage to buy you the stocks of your opted firm.

The second is for those who have little know-how and knowledge about the system of stocks and their trade. Such people would prefer to have an advisor or an agent who can process for them. He might not only advise them about which share would be more profitable to invest in, but would also offer other services like managing their low-cost investments. For this kind of approach, you shouldn't be roaming around looking for a good advisor, because almost all brokerage firms offer this service to their clients. They pick the stocks all by themselves, considering your specific goals and invest your money there.

Before moving on, you are required to make up your mind and make your final decision about which approach would be perfect for you.

2. Open an investing account

Usually, when you plan to invest in stocks, the first thing you would need is an investment account. For those who are carrying with everything on their own, a brokerage account would be a suitable one. And for those who need help and guidance, opening an account with the help of their advisor would be a sensible option.

3. Know the difference between individual stocks and exchange-traded funds

If you have opted to do all the stuff of investment and managing stocks all by yourself, then it is going to create some real difficulties for you. But don't worry, we'll figure it out for you. The first tip for you is never to forget that you don't have to complicate things and keep your stock investing simple. When it comes to investing in the stock market, you need to choose between these two types of investments, exchange-traded funds, and individual stocks.

An exchange-traded fund is a type of mutual fund that allows you to purchase smaller chunks of various stocks in just one transaction. It tracks an index and is also traded on a stock exchange like other individual stocks. In fact, from purchasing to selling, they are very much like the regular stocks sold on the stock exchange market. Moreover, they help you to build a diversified investment portfolio, as it allows you to enjoy a small share of ownership in multiple companies at the same time.

Individual stocks are preferable shares, especially for those who are new in this market. Furthermore, if you are tracking only a single firm or are interested only in buying one company's shares, then this might prove to be the safest or less risky form of investment. With this, if you wish to build a diversified portfolio, then you should definitely have a vast sum for investment and plenty of time.

4. Set a budget for your dividend stock investment

There are two most commonly and frequently asked questions by new and inexperienced investors that we are going to answer in this step:

- The first question is, what is the minimum amount of money we require to start trading? The answer to that depends on the share price or how expensive those shares are. Let's suppose that you are planning to invest in the form of exchange-traded funds; in such cases, the minimum amount you need is only a hundred dollars or sometimes even less than that.
- The second question is, what is the ideal amount of money I should invest? We have also mentioned it before how much you invest is completely your personal preference. You can invest a large share of your savings altogether at the same time for a diversified portfolio, or you can invest whole finance in the form of smaller chunks from time to time as you gain more understanding about the market.
- Investing a large sum is recommended when you have planned for the long-term, and you are not concerned about the short-term returns. But if you are talking about individual stocks, then we would recommend you to keep less than 10 percent of your portfolio.

5. Start investing

You can begin with your investment after you have completed the steps mentioned above. But it would be much better if you could also determine some tactics and approaches. They play an important role in guiding you towards the right share and can help you in maximizing the return. Many experts recommend that try to build a bulky portfolio with limited finance, and if you believe and are certain about the potential long-term growth of the firm, then always go for choosing individual stocks.

Now that you are fully prepared, so let's consider the two ways of investing in more detail. The two ways include exchange-traded funds and individual dividend stocks.

Investing in Dividend Stocks through ETFs

Dividends ETF, being related to the same type, contain dividend stocks from multiple firms willing to sell their shares on the market. It is considered to be the shortest and safest way of having a wide investment portfolio and for your payout too. Shortest in a way that it requires far less time to invest in ETF than in individual dividend stocks and safest because there is less risk involved in it.

It helps when any of the firms you have invested in stop paying dividends. But when you have multiple sources, then there is nothing to worry about. Moreover, keep one thing in mind that whenever you are buying the dividend stocks, set a safe payout in your top priorities.

How to Invest in Dividend Stock through ETF

- Try to find a dividend ETF with dividend stocks of

various firms. For this, you can also scroll your broker's website. Most probably, you should go for the safest low-cost dividend stocks. Moreover, you are required to filter your search for shares and only consider those options which are commission-free. This way, you can save your funds and can maximize the amount invested.
- Before making a final decision, you should completely analyze the ETF. It is to make sure that that you are going to invest in stocks and not in bonds. Not only this, but you might also need to keep an eye on the following:
    o The dividend yield or the percentage you will receive in the form of dividends each year, in return of the amount you have invested. The higher this percentage, the more beneficial it will be. However, in the case, if it is higher than 3.5 percent, then you might need to analyze it more precisely to assess the safety of your investment.
    o The period of return should also be as high as possible. The minimum return period set by most companies is of 5 years.
    o Look for the expense ratio. It is an annual fee that you are liable to pay or is deducted from the amount you will receive as a dividend. It is recommended that the expense ratio should be 0.5 percent or even less than that, or else you might end up earning less than the amount you initially invested.

- Now that you have fully examined the ETF and have considered its advantages before making a final decision, you can buy it just like you buy a stock using your investment account. For more investment in the same ETF, you can add more money to it regularly.

Investing in Individual Dividend Stocks

If you are building an investment portfolio, you must put in your maximum effort and give it as much of your time as possible, or else it might get more complex for you. To make it less intricate, you can opt for investing using a dividend ETF, but it might not provide you the freedom of choosing your preferred dividend stocks and might not allow you to make changes in your portfolio. On the other hand, when you are investing individually, you have access to all such options.

Nevertheless, before purchasing any stock, you should always analyze the company issuing those shares, its past and current performance, and how much risk is involved in the investment. After this, you can determine how much you want to invest in it. Following are the steps that guide you about how to buy a dividend stock:

- First of all, find a stock with a regular payout. Many financial sites can provide you with the required information and details about the stock and its dividends by different limited companies. Brokerage websites might also provide you with assistance in finding the relevant details.
- Before finalizing on a company, you first need to

analyze it, and this might be the most difficult step. But the final decision should only be made once you understand its past, current, and future forecasted financial position. It is necessary to determine and choose a healthy company to ensure that they would be able to pay a dividend for a much longer period. You might also need a company's financial statements to help you with this step.
- Finally, at last, you have to decide how many shares you should be buying. If you want to make an investment portfolio, then you should also decide how much each stock will contribute to your portfolio. For instance, if you plan to buy 25 stocks, then each stock will contribute 4 percent in your portfolio.

CHAPTER TWO

DIVIDEND INVESTING FOR NEW INVESTORS

Beginner's Guide to Dividend Investing

Generating passive income for the rest of your life without having to work for money actively is a tempting idea. However, the road to financial security is long and challenging. It involves a variety of investment strategies, some of which may be extremely risky. Having said that, dividend investing is one of the least risky investment strategies most investors employ to secure their future financially.

As an investment strategy, dividend investing appeals to many people, yet there is a lot to learn before you begin building wealth by investing your money in dividend stocks. This is a comprehensive guide on how to invest in dividend stocks as a novice investor.

How to Get Started

While it's true that a lot of people make money by investing in stocks, it is also possible to lose money really quickly if you don't know what you're doing and make all the wrong moves. Therefore, you must do thorough research before you dive into dividend investing. According to Warren Buffet, in investing, if you don't strike, you don't score. In other words, you have to give it your best shot if you want to succeed.

Novice investors are usually hesitant about investing in stocks at the very beginning. As an alternative, you can start by purchasing shares of mutual funds and ETFs – a shared fund where another company makes investments in different stock classes, and you get a share in the returns. Once you are more confident and ready to take the next step, invest in dividend stocks.

Dividend Stocks

A business that has stable cash flow and is capable of sustaining its profitability declares dividends. The company experiences a certain growth period, during which it reinvests the profits in the company so it could generate more profits and ultimately benefit investors, either in the form of stock appreciation or higher dividend payouts. As soon as the company makes its dividend payments to investors, they can choose to either reinvest those dividends by buying more shares of the same stock or invest their money elsewhere.

Dividend Investing

Dividend investing is about building a collection of safe stocks that pay regular dividend yields. These dividend payouts generate income throughout the year and add to your wealth. Dividend investors can have their dividend income deposited into their brokerage account through which the money can be transferred to their regular bank account.

If you invest enough in dividend stocks, you can earn some serious amount of money every quarter of a year. This will eventually contribute to making your investments more lucrative and adding to your wealth.

The overwhelming popularity of dividend stocks is due to higher returns and stock appreciation. Investors find dividends appealing because dividend payout rates are usually higher than interest rates. Then there's a chance that the stocks may appreciate in value over time, which will ultimately benefit you when you decide to sell your share of the stock.

Even the smartest of investors do not agree on whether or not dividend investing is a fool-proof strategy to amass wealth. However, there are some definite advantages to dividend investing.

- **Dividend Stocks Shield You from the Fluctuations of the Stock Market**

Investment in dividend stocks may have its own set of pros and cons, but it cannot be denied that it provides you a safety shield from the varying trends of the stock market. While the next uptrend or downtrend cannot be predicted with any accuracy, dividend stocks keep you from second-guessing the movements of the stock market.

The trends in the stock market fluctuate because investors are constantly trying to outperform the market using technical analysis and calculated guesses. Investors' demands and cash flow of large corporations is what causes the stock market to fluctuate. And despite your most dedicated efforts, it is highly impossible to predict these movements in advance.

As a new investor, it can be difficult to pick the right stocks every time constantly. Sometimes, the stocks you invest in may depreciate in value; sometimes, their prices will increase as people continue to try to predict the future of the stock market so they could take actions to make their investments more profitable.

- **Varied Fluctuation in Dividend Stocks**

Dividends do not always fluctuate, similar to how the stock market does. Every quarter of a year, investors make presumptions about dividend stocks and fluctuations in payouts. A variety of factors contribute to changes in a company's dividend payout and stock price fluctuations.

New-born business ventures that are in the growth phase believe their quickly growing stock price would convince the investors into spending money to buy their company's stocks. As a result of this, the dividend payout rates offered by such companies are extremely low. On the other hand, companies with weaker financial footing and fewer resources offer high dividend payouts. They want to keep the investors' money so they can recover their losses and have enough investment to rebuild their company's reputation.

An investor's job is to look for a company that has reliable cash flow and can continue to pay dividends without making cuts in the payouts.

- **Dividends Provide a Reliable Stream of Passive Income**

    Conventional stock market gains fluctuate too rapidly and too unpredictably to offer any kind of reliability to the investors. Dividend stock investors, on the other hand, can grow their dividend portfolio without having to worry about constant fluctuation in stocks.

    In the case of dividend investments, growth compounding can help you grow your wealth faster by reinvesting your money into more shares of the stock. Compounding interest refers to how the dividend interest multiplies when you reinvest in shares of the same stock.

    The rule of seventy-two brilliantly exhibits the effect of compounding. According to this rule, the investor takes the percentage value of their dividends, divide the value by number eight, and the outcome they get is the total number of years it may take them to compound their wealth into double the initial investment.

    During the financial crisis, having a saving account that offers meager interest rates is a tedious approach to working toward financial independence. Investors need a strategy that could potentially double their money and yield fruitful results.

    Dividend stocks are an attractive investment opportunity for beginners as well as seasoned investors. They provide an authentic and steady stream of passive income to the investors.

    Here's how:

- Dividend payouts are deposited into your account on a date you could predict a few months prior.
- There's always a chance they would appreciate in stock value, and they make for a more reliable income than investment in real estate or bonds.
- They provide investors with a sum of money they could live off of for long periods of time.

Investors not looking for a lump-sum payout on their investments value the idea of having a fixed amount of money being deposited into their accounts every quarter. Dividends bring in a steady source of income, which could replace your employment income and help you reach your ultimate financial goal safely.

How to Pick a Company for Dividend Investing?

Once you have decided that you are ready for dividend investing, it's time for research. Dividend-paying companies are usually safe choices, yet nothing in the stock market comes with a guarantee, and you must make smart choices. Some businesses have hit a plateau in terms of growth and stability. These companies are excellent options for dividend investing because they offer the financial security that many newbies fail to deliver.

Example

Let's take the example of McDonald's. When you invest in MCD, you do it with the conviction that this fast-food chain is not going to go out of business anytime soon. Since MCD is a giant corporation that makes more than enough to reinvest and still have some money, it pays out in dividends.

Since investing in dividend-paying stocks is comparatively low risk, they appeal to young investors to generate a substantial income over time. On the other hand, people approaching the age of retirement also find corporations like MCD an attractive investment because they want a steady stream of passive income for the rest of their retirement years.

Build a Dividend Stock Portfolio

Investment in a single dividend stock is the fast lane to financial downfall. Even the ones that look like promising business prospects have their ups and downs, and their stocks could dive.

Let's take Netflix as an example. This company went through some trouble in the years 2011 and 2012 when it hiked up its rates. Now if you had spent all your money in Netflix in 2010, hoping for miraculous growth and had to sell your shares by 2012, you would have gotten a tiny bit of growth out of making the sale, but nothing as compared to how much you would make had you still had the shares today.

Here's what this scenario teaches us:

- Never invest all of your money in a single venture. This is a rookie mistake and can cause you a lot of financial problems. Most seasoned investors have an extremely diversified portfolio comprising of different stock investments. Investment in a variety of stocks will lead you to have different financial goals and expectations from each of them. Besides keeping you from a financial disaster, a diversified portfolio expands your options to grow your wealth. So, if you find two appealing companies you'd like to invest in, don't pick one. Invest in both.

- Never second guess the stock market. Even the ones that may seem to be promising business prospects could go down in value, and the most unsuspecting ones could rise to the top. Again, taking Netflix as an example, the company lost 81k subscribers in 2011 when it raised its prices, and the stock price for Netflix dived. However, today Netflix has 37.6 million subscribers and is doing pretty well by the numbers, yet the stock prices fell by 60% in the span of a few months. This explains that stock prices remain volatile to trends in the stock market no matter how stable the company looks on paper.
- Short-term investments often do more harm than they do good. Netflix's stock price has had some serious fluctuations over the years. People who invested in the company for a long time were able to reap the benefits of stock growth Netflix has shown in recent years. However, if your goal was to buy and sell, and you couldn't stick around when Netflix's stock prices fell, you ended up faring much worse. So, if stock volatility is hard for you to handle, you're better off not investing in growth businesses.

Another such company is Apple. The year following the death of Steve Jobs, Apple's stock price experienced a significant drop in monetary value. In spite of that, the company's stocks are still priced higher now than they were at the beginning of 2012, and it has started making dividend payouts. Ultimately, it is important to do your research on the health of the company before buying shares of stock, and once you do make a purchase, stick around for the long run.

In the words of Warren Buffet:

"I try to buy stock in businesses that are so wonderful that an idiot can run them. Because sooner or later, one will."

Eventually, this mentality can help you make wise decisions regarding all your investments in dividend stocks. Do you think the company is capable of making more money? Is there a chance that its stocks will appreciate in value? Is the company financially stable enough to not make any dividend cuts? Is there room for the company's dividend yield to grow?

If the answer to all of these questions is a yes, then you have reason to invest and add the company to your stock portfolio. However, don't hurry into making a purchase. Take your time, invest some time and effort into research, and consider all your options before you decide on one.

CHAPTER THREE

Taxation on Dividend Investment

How is Dividend Income Taxed?

The investment income that is generated through stocks and by mutual funds is known as dividends.

Qualified Dividends

A qualified dividend is one that is taxed similar to capital gains but at a lower tax rate than the one used on the regular personal income of an individual. However, there's a catch. To benefit from this special tax rate, the dividend must be paid by a US-based company, a foreign company operating in the US, or a foreign company's share of stock that can be traded on the US stock market easily.

Understanding Qualified Dividends

Investors love receiving dividend income, yet when it comes to paying taxes, they are always looking for tax cuts and deductions. Those making their investments outside of tax-favored accounts like the Individual Retirement Account (IRA) must understand the taxation on their dividend income.

While dividend income is taxed, some types of dividends are favored by the US tax laws and are taxed at a comparatively lower rate than other types of income. The dividend tax rates in the US range from 0% to 20% of the individual's annual dividend income.

The dividend stock must be held for a time period longer than 60 days during the holding period of 121 days that begins 60 days prior to the ex-date to meet the requirements for the low tax rate on dividends. This means that stock traders who buy and sell stock in the span of a few days have to pay a regular tax rate. Similarly, if the dividends are due in a time period that exceeds 366 days, the stock should be held for more than 90 days during the holding period of 181 days that starts 90 days prior to the date the ex-date.

- Those who earn less than a sum total of $39,375 annually or are in the 10% and 12% tax brackets do not have to pay taxes on the dividend income.
- Individuals in 22%, 24%, 32%, and 35% tax brackets have to pay their taxes at a 15% tax rate.
- Those with an income that exceeds $434,500 or tax brackets of 35% or 37% pay 20% of their annual income in taxes.

Non-Qualified Dividends

Non-qualified dividends are those that do not qualify for the lower tax rates and are taxed at a rate applied to an individual's regular income. These dividends do not meet the specific requirements for qualified dividends and are treated by the IRS (Internal Revenue Service) as short term capital gains.

Irrespective of your tax bracket, you will be paying a significantly higher amount of money in taxes if your dividend income does not meet the requirements of a qualified dividend.

Qualified Dividends vs. Non-Qualified Dividends – The Big Difference

The difference between qualified vs. non-qualified dividends may seem to be a minor one, yet it casts a significant impact on the overall income of an investor. Most dividends paid by companies based in the US are qualified dividends, and investors can benefit from the special tax rates applied on the income yielded from these dividends.

The major difference between qualified and non-qualified dividends is the rate at which these dividends are taxed. Qualified dividends have a preferred rate, whereas non-qualified dividends are given the regular tax treatment. Individuals in any tax bracket can see the difference between tax rates depending on whether or not they have qualified dividends or non-qualified ones.

Requirements for Qualified Dividends

Here are a few requirements an investment stock eligible for qualified dividend taxation must meet:

Criteria for Foreign Companies

A foreign company that meets the requirements of a qualified dividend must satisfy one of the following three conditions:

- The company is based in the US.

- The company is eligible for tax benefits under the US tax treaty.
- The stock of the company is tradable on the US stock market.

A foreign business corporation that is considered a passive foreign investment company is not eligible for qualified dividend taxation.

Exempted Dividend Stocks

Some dividends, without any further evaluation, are exempted from the list of stocks considered for qualified dividend taxation. These exempted dividends include Real Estate Investment Trusts (REITs), Master Limited Partnerships (MLPs), Dividends on employee stock options, and those coming from tax-exempt organizations.

Moreover, dividends from deposits in savings banks, credit unions, or other financial organizations are not considered qualified dividends and are to be filed as interest income. In addition to these, special one-time dividends also remain non-qualified.

The Impact of Qualified Dividends on Investors

For most investors, whether or not their dividends are qualified or not is not something they spend hours pondering over because most of the dividends issued by US-based companies are qualified dividends. However, investors who take an interest in buying shares in foreign stock, REITs, MLPs, and other types of investments discussed above do not get to reap the benefits of special tax rates.

There is not much an investor can do to have their dividend income considered as qualified. The maximum an investor can do is to hold stocks for the duration of the minimum holding period so they could file their investment returns as qualified dividends.

How to Report Dividend Income on a Tax Return?

Dividend income is to be reported on Form 1040. If your dividend income exceeds $1,500 or if you receive dividends on behalf of someone else because they have nominated you, you must also file Schedule B. Reporting dividend income on your tax return is a simple process, made even easier when you are using an online tax software to help you select the correct forms and fill them out accurately.

What is a Schedule B Form?

Schedule B is a tax form investors use to list their interest and dividend income sources in addition to their regular income. It is compulsory to fill Schedule B if the income generated by interest or your investment in dividend stocks is more than $1,500.

You can also use Schedule B to make a list and review your interest and dividend sources before you report them on Form 1040.

Other Taxes

Having a steady stream of dividend income can also trigger Additional Medicare Tax (AMT). This tax is paid in addition to the income tax you pay on your dividends. Here are two conditions that prompt AMT:

- If you are single and have a Modified Adjusted Gross Income (MAGI) of at least $200,000.
- If you are a married couple and your MAGI exceeds $250,000.
- If you a married but file a separate tax return than your spouse, the threshold for MAGI is $125,000.

In the cases mentioned above, the US government charges you with a 0.9% Medicare Tax on your net investment income.

The Net Investment Income Tax

The Net Investment Income Tax – or NIIT – is a comparatively higher tax levied at a rate of 3.8%. This tax is triggered when your Additional Medicare Tax kicks in, or you reach the threshold for your net investment income.

You must know that all taxable dividend income is filed under investment income even if your dividends are non-qualified and are charged at ordinary tax rates.

The Bottom Line

As discussed earlier, most dividend-paying corporations based in the US are qualified for special dividend tax rates. So investors must not worry about the marginal differences between the two. When it comes to dividend investing, however, the investor must be well-informed about the tax implications and rates incurred by their dividend income, especially when they are large enough to make a huge cut in your profit returns. To thoroughly understand qualified and non-qualified dividends and their impact on taxation, the investors must communicate with their broker or accountant.

Ways to Avoid Taxation on Dividends and Capital Gains

An increase in income – whether active or passive – always adds to your tax bracket. Investment returns of short-term capital gains and non-qualified dividends are taxed with your personal income, so it is awfully tricky to avoid taxation on those. However, long-term capital gains (LTCG) and qualified dividends (QD) fall into a different variety and can be more favorable flavors of investment for taxpayers.

Although taxes on these investments are usually lower than income taxes, you can expect to pay at least 15% or as much as 37% on them. Besides the 15% standard tax, following taxes apply on your qualified dividends and long-term capital gains:

- 3.8% Net Investment Income Tax (also called ACA surtax) for individuals whose Adjusted Gross Income (AGI) is at least $200,000, or couples with a minimum AGI of $250,000.
- An additional 5% tax for individuals who fall into the top federal tax bracket.
- State Income Tax, may go up to as high as 13.3%.

Taxable accounts that have income from dividend stocks rolling in are looking at some heavy taxation, irrespective of whether or not they fall into the top federal tax bracket.

Methods to Avoid Taxation on Passive Earnings

Individuals with a taxable income that falls below the threshold of $38,601 and married couples earning a total taxable income below the cut off $77,200 have an opportunity to build a long-term portfolio of dividend growth stocks and those with remarkable dividend yields. In Warren Buffet's words – buy and hold.

Families that are far wealthier with children aged 18 or above can lower their estate taxes so they could benefit from the Annual Gift Tax Exclusion (AGTE) by transferring their shares of dividend stocks into their children's names. Assuming the children are young and a lot less wealthy than their parents, the transfer of shares will not trigger deferred taxes. As a result, even with the ownership of their new stocks, the children's annual taxable income will fall below the threshold, and the dividend income they receive from those stocks will be tax-free.

Example

Now, consider that a wealthy businessman lives in New York and is in the top federal tax bracket. His dividend payouts are taxed at a federal tax rate of 23.8%, 3.8% of which is the Obamacare dividend tax. Besides this 23.8%, he will also have to pay state and local taxes at the rates of 8.8% and 3.9%, respectively. This makes the total taxable percentage amount to be 36.5%.

To avoid paying taxes, this businessman transfers some of his shares of dividend stocks to his married son residing in Dallas, Texas. The son is only now starting his own business and one which currently generates no income. Suppose that his wife makes a total of $50,000 a year. Even with his wife's income, the couple does not reach the $77,200 tax exemption threshold. Now, as per Texas state tax law, the residents are not charged a state income tax. Taking this into account and the fact that the dividend income from his father's shares remains untaxed until it crosses the $77,200 limit, a lot of money that was previously going to go into the pockets of the IRS will now remain in the family.

In addition to these, there are four more ways how you can avoid taxation on dividend income and capital gains:

1. Keep Your Taxable Income Low

Earn what you can but avoid turnover in your taxable account. How?

It's fairly simple. Buy and hold the stock. If a substantial amount of your dividend income is taxable, and in Roth dollars (tax-free dollars until used), you will be able to keep your taxable income way below your annual budget.

As per 2018 standards, the threshold for tax-free income for a couple was $77,200 on all long-term capital gains and qualified dividends. Now, the threshold may come across as low, but carefully divided income and a well-constructed, diversified portfolio can help a couple spend a six-figure income while keeping their taxable income low.

Comparatively, if you are a single filer, you can only keep half of the taxable income in 0% LTCG and QD bracket. For individuals amassing a good amount of wealth, keeping taxable income under $37,650 is a difficult task. Since marriage divides your wealth, it can be an effective solution to keeping taxable income below the threshold.

2. Tax-Loss Harvesting and Tax-Gain Harvesting

Tax-Loss Harvesting and Tax-Gain Harvesting are two tax strategies that could reduce the investor's tax bills.

Tax Loss Harvesting

Harvesting losses is an effective year-end tax-reducing strategy, especially if you are generating passive income through long-term capital gains and dividend stocks. Some tax rates on capital gains run as high as 20% in addition to the 3.8 income surtax we discussed earlier.

The tax-loss harvesting strategy is used to offset gains in securities experiencing a loss. You can use any remaining loss to offset a maximum of $3,000 of your earned income. Any remaining losses will be compensated in the succeeding years.

Tax-Gain Harvesting

Unlike tax-loss harvesting, tax-gain harvesting is a strategy in which you sell winning securities to capture capital gains. Now, why would you do that since those capital gains could also increase your tax liability?

Tax-gain harvesting is not for every investor. You only use this strategy when your current capital gains tax rate is far lower than what you deduce it will be in the future. In other words, you sell a winning investment now and pay the tax instead of having to pay higher taxes in the future.

Tax-gain harvesting is a good strategy to utilize in early retirement. If you are lucky enough not to have hit the magic figure of ($77,200 for joint filers) yet, you can take some capital gains to reset your cost basis without having to pay tax. You can do this until you hit the threshold.

Another way to do this is to make Roth conversions –

whichever works better for you. Even if you go over the threshold by a few hundred dollars, don't worry. You will only be taxed 15% on the LTCG and QD for the meager overage and not for the total of your income.

3. Donate Appreciated Investments

It may not be the most attractive way to get tax reductions, but it is one of the most effective and least complicated ones. Donating appreciated assets dissolves taxation levied on the capital gains. Neither you nor the receiver will have to pay the taxes.

Moreover, donations not only make you feel as if you are giving back to the community by contributing your wealth, but also make you feel good about being successful and influential. Giving stocks directly to a charity can be an unwieldy task. It is better to make use of the Donor Advised Fund to facilitate such transactions.

4. Death

When you die, assets in a taxable account are passed on to the heirs in the next generation. This transference of assets resets the cost basis to the current value. The assets can then be sold without having to pay any taxes. This results in a huge tax break.

CHAPTER FOUR

Passive Income

What Are the Three Major Types of Income?

As an investor, it is important to understand the different types of income, so you know exactly how you want to make more money before you begin investing. When people talk about income sources, they often overlook the fact that there is more than one way to earn income. They speak of it as if it's all just the same.

On the contrary, the type of income you make largely affects how much time and effort you invest into making money. Understanding the difference between different sources of income is essential to choose the one that fits your financial requirements the best.

Moreover, being able to differentiate between different income sources will help you employ a combination of these income ideas to create a consistent influx of cash every month. While it may be time-consuming to try out different income ideas, combining a side business with a passive income source and returns from your investments can ultimately make huge contributions to making you wealthier and sustaining your financial health.

Three Major Types of Income

Following are the three major types of income and how you can earn them:

Active Income

Active income also termed as earned income, is when you exchange your time and effort for money. You put in diligent work and exchange, get paid by your employer.

Some major examples of active income are wages, salaries, bonuses, creators, producers, traders, etc.

Tax Implications for Active Income

Earned income has a comparatively higher tax rate than other pays, ranging from 10%-35%, besides Medicare, Social Security, etc. However, as per tax reforms in 2018, the top taxpayers fell from a whopping 39.6% to 37%.

Characteristics of Active Income

Active Income alone cannot make you rich. For one, it has an elevated tax rate. Secondly, it can only be earned by working long hours, a lot of which – assuming you are paid incredibly well – is given away in taxes.

Another disadvantage, other than charges or assessments, is that once you quit working, the money stops coming in. On the upside, earned compensation is the least overwhelming and draining kind of pay you could make. You can find another profession or side occupation easily enough in the US to make cash on the side and earn profits.

Types of Active Income

- **A Creator**

A creator generates income by making something that is in demand. A woodworker, performer, author, manufacturer, and rancher are all examples of a creator. A creator produces goods – in effect, creating them – rather than simply providing a service.

There are two types of goods:

Tangible Goods

These are the goods you can physically touch or feel.

Intangible Goods

These are the goods that you cannot physically touch or feel.

Examples of tangible goods include furniture items, electronic appliances, or buildings, which we also often refer to as manufacturing. Tangible goods also include things that come from primary or the most basic sources like eggs, vegetables, fruits, and grains, etc.

Intangible goods – also termed as intellectual property – are things like books, movies, videos, audios, articles, and software, etc. All the things that hold value, yet cannot be touched or felt are intangible goods brought into existence by a creator.

A creator, whether he creates tangible or intangible goods, creates something in demand by using other source materials or sometimes creates things from scratch. This makes a creator different from other types of active income because goods produced by a creator can be sold or used to generate an income.

- **A Worker**

A worker actively generates income by working. This is what many people refer to as 'active income' in the literal sense.

However, it includes investing your energy like using your skills, information, and experience to complete a task. In any case, you are merely accomplishing something for another person.

- **A Teacher**

You can generate income by teaching a topic or skill such as by private tutoring, an academic course, or a professional degree.

Some people teach you things that are not valid, yet that you might need to hear. Training information and abilities are consistently accessible, especially if they are an exceptional sort of intelligence or aptitude that very few individuals know or some skill in demand.

Teaching or instructing is only moving information or transferring a skill but could help you earn extra income.

Passive Income

Passive income is generated by your assets, where you are not actively working.

The examples of passive income are rental income, business income, or income generated by selling an intellectual property.

Tax Implications for Passive Income

Passive income receives favorable taxation, including special tax rates, to propel financial growth.

The Characteristics of Passive Income

Passive income is thought to be the key to building wealth. Once you have an investment that generates recurring income, you don't have to do much to maintain it (so time is not a limitation).

Typically, there isn't much of a start-up cost you need to provide to begin earning passive income. For instance, you can invest your time to create a business, or you can get investors to fund your ventures or invest in your real estate properties. It's not as simple as earning active income, yet it's hardly as challenging as portfolio income. It takes a lot of investment to generate portfolio income, but you can generate a lot of passive income with comparatively fewer amounts of money.

Types of Passive Income

Passive income sources are the most misconstrued and mishandled sources on the web. Everybody cherishes procuring a salary without taking any kind of action, and that draws out the con artists. Also referred to as residual income, this kind of income helps you earn money from things like rent and royalties.

- **Self-Publishing**

By far, self-publishing is the most preferred source of passive income. For creative individuals, photography or painting would make for an excellent source of passive income. Regardless of whether or not you're regularly creating more content, self-publishing can provide you with a steady stream of income.

- **Working as an Artist**

Being an artist doesn't mean you need to be a Picasso to bring home the bacon. Sites like Patreon make it simple to get patrons for your work, and many other sites and platforms help you sell your photographs and music.

- **Renting a Room in Your Home**

Renting a room does not make for a source of income you could rely on forever, yet it is another way to make money without having to work for it actively. It probably won't be something you rake in tons of cash from, but it's an easy way to generate passive income. If you are thinking about leasing a room, keep high requirements for roommates. It's better to let a place sit empty than to give it to somebody who'd be a nuisance.

- **Cash Back Shopping**

Cashback shopping is one of the most disputed sources of passive income, primarily because it could yield a few hundred dollars a month if used correctly. Websites like TopCashBack are used to search for rebate programs, and cash-back offers for things you were to purchase anyway.

This website has direct links to the retailer of the products, so you get the deals and offers given to others plus a 5% to 20% cashback opportunity. However, cashback shopping works on the human psyche a lot as a discount tag or sale does. When you see the sale tag, you spend money you weren't otherwise going to spend and purchase things you weren't otherwise going to buy. Similarly, cashback offers can tempt you into spending more than you originally planned to.

Ultimately, 15% cashback on a $100 article still means you are spending $85 that would have otherwise stayed in your wallet.

Portfolio Income

Portfolio income is money acquired through returns on capital gains. This type of income is also referred to as capital income.

For instance, suppose an individual makes a stock purchase in a corporation and plans on selling his share of the stock at a higher price in the future. So, if they make the purchase the stock for $10 today and sell it for $40 a few months later, they get $30 as capital gains. This is precisely what portfolio income is – making profits via capital gains. This is the method stock traders use to generate large sums of money. They invest in stocks they feel are sold for less than they're actually worth with the expectation that stock prices will soar in the future. When that happens, they sell their stocks for capital gain.

Some examples of portfolio income are:

1. Exchange of resources, similar to stocks, securities, and shared assets.

2. Purchasing and selling land.

3. Purchasing and selling different supplies, such as a vehicle.

Tax Implications for Portfolio Income

Portfolio pay is taxed at 10%-20% for securities held for more than a year and exhausted as earned salary whenever held under a year. In any case, portfolio salary isn't taxed for Medicare or Social Security. Taxation on capital gains can be offset if you face losses in any of your other investments.

The Characteristics of Portfolio Income

One drawback of portfolio income is that for an average individual, making contributions or investments before they can reap the profits is a challenging and intimidating prospect. For this reason alone, many individuals avoid going for portfolio income. Moreover, this sort of income may take years to generate if you understand the investing concepts that require investors to buy and hold the stock for years

In case you're a dealer and endeavor to do it a lot quicker, you should be great at it because it's very similar to betting. If you are a stock trader, you'd want to sell the stock and make money much faster. This incurs a very high risk of failure, and you must have excellent intuition and research skills to successfully second guess the market and generate income through capital gains. This method of earning is a lot like gambling. Only the stakes are a lot higher.

To successfully generate portfolio income, you must have enough money to be able to make upfront investments. This is a major reason why people do not want to invest. You can do it another way by starting with a small investment and then making regular contributions to it. However, that too requires you to have a capital sum.

Types of Portfolio Income

Following are some examples of portfolio income:

- **A Certificate of Deposit (CD)**

A certificate of deposit or fixed-term deposit is a kind of investment fund that matures after a fixed time period at a specific interest rate. Most certificates of deposit come with investment requirements kept to a minimum.

- **Savings Accounts**

Saving accounts are, in some ways, very similar to CDs. But in contrast to CDs, they do not have a fixed holding period.

- **US Saving Bonds**

US savings bonds are generally safe investment funds that pay you interest for up to 30 years. Issued and backed by the credit standing of the US government, saving bonds is one of the most common forms of investment in the US.

- **Money Market Accounts**

This is another form of saving product. MMAs comprise of short-term but high-quality investments.

- **Municipal and Corporate Bonds**

State and local governments issue municipal bonds. Through these bonds, the government borrows money and uses it to fund its operations. Corporate bonds are issued by companies seeking to borrow money from their investors.

- **Peer-to-Peer Lending (P2P)**

P2P is to borrow money directly from other individuals. This way, you can cut out conventional financial institutions from the lending process.

- **Preferred Stocks**

These are hybrid securities meaning they have characteristics that are a mix of bonds and common stocks.

- **Dividend-Paying Common Stocks**

These stocks are similar to dividend stocks, except they provide partial ownership to the investor in a dividend-paying company.

- **Mutual Funds**

Open-end mutual funds, closed-end mutual funds, and exchange-traded funds, all have varying characteristics. But eventually, they all are similar in that they offer the investor to expand their field of operation across a class of assets.

- **Real Estate Investment Trusts (REITs)**

REITs are for companies that own, manage, or finance real estate that generates income. These companies issue dividend-paying common stock to the general public for investment.

- **Master Limited Partnerships**

    MLPs are a business venture similar to a limited partnership except that their stocks are traded publicly. Like REITs, MLPs issue dividend-paying common stocks to the public.

    The above discussed are the types and subtypes of income. All of these classifications describe how different forms of income work and how we can earn through them. These classifications will help you to understand and differentiate between different types of income and incorporate them into your investment strategies and financial plans.

What is Passive Income?

Passive income is when a person's earnings are derived from such operations or activities in which that person was not actively a part of it or was not physically involved. These operations might include investing in a limited partnership, return on investment from rental property, and other forms of enterprises.

Other than passive income, there are other types of income, as well as active income and portfolio income. Like active income, passive income is also taxed by the local, state, and the federal government. Many experts and analysts consider portfolio income to be a form of passive income too. It is because the dividends and interest received on investment are also a way of earning passive income.

Some popular sources of passive income are investing in real estate, peer-to-peer lending (also called P2P), and dividend stocks. Individuals who earn passive income are likely to be associated with receiving interest on savings, investments in industries, and rapidly-growing business ventures, gains, or surplus made on the sale of assets and shares. Unemployment benefits can also generate passive income, the pay an employee receives once he or she retires, a lucky draw or lottery, capital gains, and freelance opportunities.

23 Ways to Earn Passive Income

There is no secret or magic trick that you would require to convert your precious time into money. Rather you just need to sow your seeds in the form of investment and wait until it gets mature till the time of harvesting arrives.

Therefore, we have collectively researched and have listed down below the 23 most effective ways of investing your funds to generate a passing income for a long period.

Through Robo-Investing

As mentioned above, passive income means minimizing your involvement in the activity, which will generate revenue or the return on investment for you. Therefore, a computerized algorithm that is designed to manage your funding or investment is the clearest example of passive income that you might find in today's time.

Robo-advisors are classified as an automated investment advisor who is 21/7 available to provide you with the best assistance regarding your financial matter, advising on when and how to manage your investments online with minimum human intervention in it. Robo-investing is also one of their primary and most preferred tools that allow you to choose how much you want to invest, and your part of the job is done.

Now let this algorithm convert your investments into a steady stream of passive income. This system charges you a fee as low as one-fourth of what you might have pay to a manager for managing your financial accounts. Moreover, it also helps you in reducing the tax brackets levied on your investment, maximizing the returns on the amount you invest.

Investing in Real Estate and Property

Many investors, whether foreign or direct, always prefer real estate investment over others. In this case, your passive income would be the leftover balance after you have deducted all the costs and expenses you might incur for owning the property from the net value of the property you have paid to acquire it. The expenses for which you necessarily have to pay for include, mortgage, the dues for HOA and other societies, rehab costs, etc.

There are multiple sources through which you can invest and manage your real estate business. I would recommend you to go through them for a better understanding and that you might also found any of your interest;

- **Fundrise**

It is an online investment platform design, especially keeping in mind the real estate industry. It is particularly designed for those living in a country where it is too expensive to buy and to own a property. Or maybe you are too busy in other legal matters and formalities that you are left with not enough time so that you can manage all your properties by yourself. In all such cases, it might appear to be the most appropriate choice to make.

It helps you raise finance for your business through crowd-funding, and provides assistance in managing those properties that give you the stabilized rent-based earning. Not only is this, but distributing profits to other investors quite easy using this platform. Before, the investment in real estate was considered as the most expensive, but since Fundrise was introduced, the circumstances have changed. You can start investing in Fundrise with only 500 dollars.

- **Roofstock**

If you are planning to become a real estate investor, but are afraid of the burden of responsibilities and management that would fall on your shoulders, then Roofstock is a potential candidate that has a clear solution to your problem. It is a platform that offers you multiple services for your business, which range from managing properties it owns to investing in stand-alone houses.

Let's suppose you want to invest in a single detached residence, then all you have to do is to put up your funding. The ownership of the property would be transferred to you, and the tenants living in it would not be disturbed at all. The difference that would occur is only that the rental income that previously someone else was receiving will now come to you.

- **Realty Mogul**

Like the two platforms mentioned above, Realty Mogul is also a financial assistance platform that helps you accumulate enough wealth for investing in the purchase of large-sized properties. The source of finance used to pool the required amount of investment is crowd-funding. The minimum amount of investment that you require for take-off is $1,000, after which you can slowly and gradually expand the size of your operations until you start investing in larger office premises, retail spaces, etc.

High-Yield Dividend Stocks

Many of you might get confused about whether to invest in dividend stocks or to prefer bank investment. Such people need to understand that once you have finished building a diversified investment portfolio of high-yield dividend stocks, then you start receiving a regular and persistent amount of passive income at a much stable annual rate. It would be much more than you might have received on depositing your investment in commercial banks.

Moreover, when investing in stocks, the chance of capital appreciation always exists there. In this case, you might be able to earn higher passive income from multiple sources without making a further investment.

High-Yield Savings Account

Many investors consider a saving account as the most boring form of investment that you would ever come across. But while they might be boring and conventional, there is no doubt they are the safest form of investment, where your principal amount is always safe, and once the certificate of investment matures, you can withdraw your invested principal amount along with the profits.

The percentage of the rate of interest, which is generally referred to as the reward on lending or saving, is determined by the state government, central planning authority, or state bank.

However, online saving accounts and platforms offer competitive interest rates to attract more savings from your side, and they don't even lock or bound your money for a long period. Another thing to keep in mind is that the rates keep on changing regularly, so if you are planning to deposit your money in a savings account, then check what the current rate of interest on savings is.

Certificate of Deposits

Certificate of deposit, in banking commonly known as CD, is a form of savings account that is federally insured and has a never-changing rate of interest along with a fixed date for the withdrawal of principal amount, generally termed as the date when the savings "matures."

Certificate of deposits is a straightforward and the most simplistic strategy of investment, and you are not required to fulfill any legal formalities to invest in it. If you have a clear goal of investing to earn passive income while you act as a sleeping partner or investor, then I guess there is no better option for you than investing in CDs, which not only is simple but safe and risk-free as well.

CDs or Certificate of Deposits are much similar to a saving account but with a higher return. Another important detail, whether it is minor or a major one it depends on you but as a matter of fact in CD you are not allowed to ask for your funds before they are matured, no matter whatever happens. The period of maturity is usually based on the time frame that you select when opening the account.

In many countries, the greater the maturity period you select, the higher the interest rate you would receive from the federally administered financial institutions.

Rent Your Car

Do you find it weird staying at some stranger's home while on travel or on vacations, or do you feel reluctant to rent out your house to a stranger? Similarly, the same happens when you own and manage a rent-a-car business. In this business, you cannot trust in the other party who wants the car, and their purpose for renting a car. There is always a possibility that they might use your car in some kind of illegal activity, for which you can be held responsible.

Thanks to many online platforms and tourism websites that have started offering these services have made this rent-a-car a not-so-scary business. However, these have cut down the profit margins for agencies that are quite expensive and not very reliable as well.

As an investor with the hope of earning a regular passive income, you can lend your car to them, and they will pay you a commission on each ride. This way, you also don't have to worry about your car or where they would take your car, as the online company would then handle all such matters.

Invest in Business

Many experienced investors give their more preference to investing in a small-sized business and its tangible assets. This is because you can see your investment grow, as that business grows and expands its size. For this form of investment, a lot of risks are involved, although it can be minimized if before investing, you choose wisely for the right entrepreneur with the right and a creative idea. And if you do so, then there is no doubt in it that in future this might prove to be a rapid multiplier for your investment.

Many online platforms and websites have been designed to bring investors and entrepreneurs closer to each other, where you can seek better ideas of starting a business and meet many experts who can guide you about the fast-growing business investments.

Refinance or Pay Down Debt

One of many ideas to increase your net worth is to review your liabilities. And reducing your debt would definitely help you out in increasing your net worth.

- **Mortgage Debt**

You, as a borrower, have to pay back interest on a mortgage loan. At times of economic recession, interest rates fall to their lowest, and that is the opportunity you can grab by refinancing your mortgage. By doing so, you can save up to 0.5 percent or maybe a bit more on your mortgage. You might be thinking that 0.5 percent saving can do nothing, but if it is accumulated, you will end up counting to thousands, which might be a lot more than any regular investment you might have hoped for.

- **Student Loan Debt**

If you have a student loan debt or a mortgage, there is a good chance you could multiply your savings. There is nothing much you have to do, just qualify for refinancing it and save as much as you can. For instance, your current interest on a loan is 7 percent, and after refinance, it gets as low as 3 percent, then you will be saving 4 percent on your loan amount.

Invest in Index Funds

You can also invest in index funds for a regular earning of a passive income. Like the purchase of limited public shares for this investment as well, you need to have an account in the stock market.

For instance, you invest your finance in a Standard & Poor's 500 Index based market; it is considered investing in a general market. It means that you are no longer required to take all the fuss on your shoulders like choosing the type of investment, managing your investment portfolio, and thinking whether or not to buy and sell the individual company shares.

Moreover, this form of investment can be made through any offline brokerage or online investment platform.

Alternative Investment

An alternative investment is an investment that you make besides investing in bonds and stocks – like investing in an entrepreneur's creative idea broadcasted on a TV show. Not only this, but investing in terms of other assets like property, agriculture, commodities, gold, art, and antiques all are listed as alternative investments. The answer to the question of how to make alternative investments is as simple as the online investment platforms.

Rent Your Space

If you are really interested in investing in real estate and property business but are looking for a simpler option to manage, then giving your free house space or any spare property on the rental basis can prove to be the simplest source of passive income earning. The introduction of online platforms like Airbnb, VRBO, and Vacasa has made it a lot easier for you to rent your property for extra income.

- **Airbnb**

Airbnb is an online platform that allows you to travel around the world without worrying about accommodation. It provides you hotels and rooms at the most affordable pricing. So if you want to rent any of your extra rooms, then the policy of Airbnb is open for you where you can charge your customers any amount, and the company takes only 3 percent of the revenue from each booking.

- **VRBO**

VRBO is the most suitable online forum for all owners who are willing to rent their property. The services offered by VRBO are beneficial for all, only it charges the owner a 5 percent and the customer a 3 percent commission on each booking. However, its policies are very flexible, and it allows you to set the rates on your terms.

- **Vacasa**

Like Airbnb and VRBO, Vacasa as well is an online company particularly designed for tourists. Moreover, it stands out in the market for its rental management services for all those who want to rent their spare property, but either doesn't have enough time for all the management or are unable to find the right tenant.

Rideshare Driving

While it may not actually be a source of passive income, it can be considered as such due to its flexible working conditions. Rideshare driving is what most of the part-time drivers on Uber and Lyft are doing right now. They drive and offer a pick and drop service while they are already out for some other work. This way, they are earning an extra income without putting up their extra efforts.

In addition to this, many full-time drivers are now offering food delivery services too. For instance, you are going to a location to drop a passenger and also deliver a food package there. So what do you think isn't it a good way of earning the twice of what you might have earned by only dropping the person on his desired location.

Peer To Peer Lending (P2P)

Peer to peer lending, commonly known as P2P is the method of investing where you meet entrepreneurs that have the potential and creative idea a startup or to expand their existing operations, you lend them your investment, and after a certain period, they return your investment along with the interest amount.

Shop, Search and Play Online

Filling online surveys and questionnaires is another easy job you can find on the internet and can earn money sitting on your warm couch, taking small sips of coffee, and surfing the web. Again, while this may not entirely be classified as a passive income source, it can be added to the same pool owing to its flexible working hours.

Online Course or Guide

This source requires you to put up a good show of your efforts in terms of an online course or a guide in which you can have a video of you explaining anything you are good at. It can be based on your passion, your interest, or what you have been studying in university life. Many teachers are selling their lessons online and generating large revenue for themselves. It is one of the broadest mediums of connecting with a wide audience to show them your unique and inspiring content.

But many of you would still be confused about what and what not to add in your online courses. Here is a list of all add-ons you can use to make your content more interesting;

- Video, voice-over, and audio lessons
- A checklist containing all the tips and steps that you might recommend in your video
- Add informative interviews of experts and qualified professionals
- Share research reports and studies

If you are not good at writing blogs or articles and recording videos, then you can try to create an online guide. To create one, all you have to do is to gather all the relevant information regarding any topic you find interesting in a guide's format and earn money by claiming for monetization through Google AdSense and membership of other various online platforms.

Outsource Your Business

Outsourcing your business can take the burden of running

it by yourself off your shoulders as well as help you earn passive income. This way, you can focus more on other tasks generating additional income for you. Moreover, if you have enough people to outsource the work, then why not opening a freelance agency? Hire some freelancers who are good with their niches and can provide excellent results. Your task would be only to deal with the clients and to pass-on the work from clients to freelancers.

The following are some big-name companies that provide a wide online platform for all freelancers to find their job of interest and business to outsource their job to skilled and experienced people.

- **CloudPeeps**

For many years this online platform is accurately and effectively performing their task of bringing businesses with potential extra work and skilled freelancers closer to each other. If you want to outsource some part of your work, then look for individuals who excel in your line of work, and you will find people for all sorts of jobs, from marketing and managing to web development, graphic designing, and maintaining financial records.

- **Fiverr**

The services and opportunities that fiver provides to its clients and freelancers are much similar to those that CloudPeeps offers. However, the only difference exists is in their interface and the way it distributes the work.

- **Guru**

It also offers the same services as the previous two companies do, but they seem to put their major emphasis on their dynamic payment methods that include hourly pay, monthly pay, recurring payments, payment as a milestone is achieved, and payment once a project is completed.

- **PeoplePerHour**

They, with the most advanced and up-to-date interface and artificial intelligence system, connect you with the perfect match who knows how to fulfill all your project requirements perfectly. They have gathered a pool of skilled and talented freelancers on a single platform.

- **Upwork**

Like all other networks, Upwork connects you with the most talented freelancers in various industries and sectors. It allows their clients and freelancers to operate and work on short-term, long-term, and recurring projects.

Cashback Credit Cards

If your credit card is still in use and you have been using it for some purchases, then seek for the credit card rewards and try to gain as many as possible. Multiple rewards and redeemable vouchers allow you to earn up to 5% back with no additional efforts required.

If you have the right credit card that gives you good cash back rewards, then you can easily get bonus offers for travel, especially at times of holidays and vacations. By doing so, you can save hundreds to thousands of dollars on each travel every year.

Advertise Your Car

Advertising your car means putting up ads to help manufacturers further their marketing campaign by advertising their product through your vehicle. You may or may not get paid for this. If you do get paid, the earnings would be considered passive income. Many firms are providing these types of opportunities, and you can easily avail them to generate extra income.

- **Carvertise**

Carvertise is an online platform that provides you an opportunity to earn up to $1300, only by taking part in an advertising campaign for which you need to advertise their product in your car. Not only this, but they also allow you to earn up to $100 every month, and you will get all this for doing nothing; just let them use your car as an ad space or board. You can visit their website or can contact them through their Facebook page to know whether they are currently operating in your area or not.

- **Wrapify**

The services Wrapify offers a much similar to those of Carvertise, but the main difference lies in the payment method. In Wrapify, your location and the mileage you travel are tracked. Therefore, the more you travel, the more ads you will receive from the company, and the better you get paid.

- **Vugo**

Vugo brings you an amazing opportunity to earn passive income. Along with ride-share driving, you can also earn money by playing games, short commercials and ads, and many other videos. This map is intelligently designed to work for drivers using Google Maps and Waze as their route guide. It enables drivers to increase their passive income earning by $200 per month, and not only this, but there is also a tip feature build in it, particularly for drivers.

Sleep Studies

You can indeed earn while you sleep. What happens is that you get paid to sleep in an area where a psychological study is conducted on you. To qualify, you should have decent health, with a sleeping schedule of up to 7 to 8 hours. Once you are accepted for it, then you probably have to pass a physical test, which will ensure that you are physically and mentally normal and qualify for the task.

However, don't forget that to qualify for this job, you will need to make some compromises and face a few challenges, like disconnecting from social media and leaving your social life behind. For, however, long the experiment continues, there will always be someone watching you until you complete your working hours. Moreover, you might be asked to sleep in positions that might be physically uncomfortable for you, but don't worry, you will get paid well for whatever you have to face during the study.

E-bates or Online Rebates

E-bates allows you to win and enjoy multiple rebates when you purchase goods from a wide range of online retailers and e-commerce businesses. All you have to do is to shop as you normally do when there is a sale on all major online brands and stores. The percentage of the amount you receive in terms of cashback could be as high as 22%. Each month you will receive your payback amount through check, PayPal, or in the form of gift cards and redeemable vouchers.

So remember this sneaky way of earning income the next time you buy an expensive item, like a refrigerator or a microwave oven, or just buy your daily groceries from an online store. Always look for as many e-bates as possible to earn good passive income.

Start a Blog

If you are looking for a really cheap, but a regular and persistent way of generating passive income, then you should consider starting to write a blog. Literally speaking, that you have no idea about how much you can earn with a good and eye-catchy content posted on a blog. You are not required to invest a lot to make a start; however, later, you might have to pay more than just a few dollars to achieve sustenance with your income. But by the time you will be required to pitch in a substantial amount of money, you will have started to generate high revenue for yourself and wouldn't mind reinvesting some of it to grow and maintain your business.

If you can consistently manage your blog, updating it regularly with freshly brewed content, then you can potentially earn a handsome amount in terms of passive income. The more time you spend uploading the posts on your blog, the more traffic will start coming in. A blog is considered the most low-cost way of generating a fast-flowing stream of passive income. At the start, you need to be patient as it takes some time to take-off. But sooner or later, it will definitely grow.

Buy a Blog

Another suitable option is to buy an already existing blog that might have been abandoned by its owner, but now you can revive it. If the blog you buy has an average amount of already existing web traffic, then it can serve you as a perfect source of passive income.

Furthermore, some sites contain evergreen content. It is a term used for that content that can generate revenue even after several years of being uploaded, and the site has been abandoned. Such an eternal content if purchased for $5000, even then as well it is a low budget deal to make.

Affiliate Marketing

Whether you decide to start a new blog or buy an existing one, if it is not affiliated, it is not an absolute source of passive income. Affiliation can serve as a technique to generate much more than regular revenue. For this, you only have to sign up and have to promote certain goods and services on your site, and in return, you will receive either a flat fee or a commission on the total amount of sales.

Many people have a misunderstanding regarding affiliate marketing that it is way too complex, but in reality, it is not as hard as you think it may be. You can avail affiliate offers through various vendors, available on websites, and other online forums. It is always suggested to promote that product which you might be interested in, or it relates to the content uploaded on your site.

CHAPTER FIVE

PASSIVE INCOME AND DIVIDEND INVESTING

Steps to Passive Income with Dividend Investing

As you may have discovered earlier, there are plenty of ways to earn passive income. You could rent out a property, earn royalties from a book or song, or earn money by outsourcing. However, the best way to earn passive income is through dividend investing. When you purchase a stock that pays dividends, all you have to do is own the stock and wait to get paid. This is a guide to spot and buy stocks of companies that pay excellent dividends.

If you incorporate these steps into your dividend investing strategy, you will soon be building streams of passive income and finally attaining financial freedom.

Step#1 – Save and Deploy

This first step is to help you gather the building blocks of your portfolio. And to do that, you must first question why you want to invest in dividend stocks in the first place. Do you want to grow your savings with time? Do you want to build a nest egg so you could retire early? Would you like to build a solid stream of passive income so you could boost your current income?

If your answer is a yes, then dividend growth investing is the perfect strategy for you!

It is important to realize that it all starts with saving money. For every dollar you earn, you must save a few cents. The money you save from your income (after paying taxes) in percentage is called a savings rate, and it is important to maintain a steady savings rate at all costs. This rate will help you determine how long it will take for you to reach financial independence.

Most financial advisors say that you must save at least 5 10% of your income. For someone looking to achieve financial freedom a little earlier in their life, that savings rate is way too low. At the very least, you should go for a 30% savings rate, more if you earn well.

On the other hand, it is an alarming situation if you are nowhere near this figure. You need to analyze your expenses and save more. Now it may seem easy enough if your earnings are high. However, if you do not have a high income, it's time to learn some saving tips!

Step#2 – Open a Brokerage Account

Now your next step is to open a brokerage account. A brokerage account is like a bank account but with access to stocks. It gives you a place to keep your money while buying and selling stocks through this account. To this day, old school brokers make their transactions over the phone or in person. However, it is much cheaper and hassle-free to trade your stocks online.

Here's how it goes:

- The first step is to pick an online broker and sign up for a brokerage account.
- The second step is to link your regular bank account to your brokerage account and transfer funds, so you have money on hand to buy stocks.
- Use the brokerage account to look for high dividend stocks and buy them. The dividend income will be deposited into your brokerage account from then onwards.
- If you need to spend your dividend income, you can transfer the dividends to your regular bank account.

In this case scenario, one very important question arises: **how to choose a broker?**

Choosing a broker eventually depends on your circumstances and financial goals. However, mentioned below are a few factors you must consider.

Do I Need a Minimum Account Balance to Open the Account?

If you already have some money sitting in your account and waiting to be paid for dividend stocks, then the minimum balance should not bother you too much. But, if you are only just starting out, this might make a difference to you.

How Much Will They Charge Me Per Stock Purchase?

Brokers charge you a fee when you buy and sell stocks.

They charge you per every stock trade, and that's how they make their money. Since you are only likely to make 2 to 3 purchases in a month, it is not surprising that brokers charge a high fee.

However, it is best to look for a broker who charges comparatively less. It is best to hire a broker who will allow you to invest in international stocks.

Step #3 – Make a Watchlist

A good stock is one that not only makes your money grow with time but also keeps increasing the dividend income it pays you.

Here are some of the requirements every good stock should meet:

A Decade Long Streak of Increasing Dividends

A company that increases its dividends every year and has been raising them for longer than a decade cares about its shareholders. While this may not be a guarantee of the future, it's a good point to start.

Understanding Your Business

There is a very simple rule: if how a company makes its profits cannot be explained on a sheet of paper, it's too complex for investment. In other words, if you do not understand how a company operates, do not invest in it. The simpler it is, the better.

Take an example of Colgate-Palmolive. They make toothpaste and hand soaps, and that's how they make their money. People buy their toothpaste, toothbrushes, and hand soaps, and they generate profits on their sales. Simple!

Minimum Dividend Yield = 3%

The dividend yield is a stock's annual dividend payment as a percentage of the stock price per share. Suppose if a share costs $100 and pays $3 in dividends each year, you will get a dividend yield of 3% each year. Ideally, you want your dividend yield to be over 3%.

However, if the company has a promising start and is bound to grow in the coming years, a slightly lower yield works, too.

Payout Ratio < 70%

A dividend payout ratio is the percentage of the company's revenue that it uses to pay in dividends. If the company's payout ratio is less than 70%, then:

- It has enough money to keep growing its business.
- It will continue to increase the amount paid in dividends, even if it goes through a rough patch for a few years.

Step#4 – Stock Price

Never rush into buying stocks, be patient. If you've found a company that looks good, dominates the market, and satisfies your requirements, then it does not mean you should buy it at any price. You need to make sure that the stock is trading at a good price to make a profitable investment.

Here are a few things you must look out for when buying stocks:

P/E Ratio

The price to earnings ratio is a simple metric you could use to find out whether the stock you are interested in is trading at a fair price or is overvalued and expensive. Now how do you calculate the P/E ratio? It's easy. Divide the stock's current price by its Earnings per Share (EPS). All good stock analysis platforms already have a column, whether they show the P/E ratio.

If the P/E ratio is less than 20, you can go ahead and buy the stock. If the ratio exceeds 20, then it means that the stock is overpriced. The lower the P/E ratio, the better it is.

Cheaper Than Its 52-Week High

This is another metric you can easily see on Google and Yahoo Finance. It shows the price range of the stock over the past 52 weeks.

It is best to focus on companies that are trading somewhere near a 52-week low and way cheaper than their 52-week high. Do not buy a stock that is any closer to its high point than 25%. For anything higher, wait for the stock prices to drop.

Step#5 – Buy, Track, & Enjoy

If the stock is trading at a good price, has a low P/E ratio, and is near its 52-week low, you're good to make a purchase.

Place a Limit Order

Log in to your brokerage account to buy the stock. Now you could buy the stock at its current price, which will fluctuate, or you could set up a limit order.

A limit order will set up a payment to trigger once the stock has reached a price you have set. As soon as the stock price reaches your given limit, the software will pull a payment trigger and buy as many shares as you stated.

Enjoy Your Dividend Income

Once you have purchased a stock, you will find dividends coming in over the next few months. When you get paid your first dividend, it feels like you have just been handed extra money. Soon the dividends will start creeping up the monetary ladder, and your dividend income will multiply.

It's time you get used to earning passive income!

Track Your Portfolio

Stocks that pay out money in dividends do not fluctuate as much as other stocks. Dividends investments do not require you to keep a close eye on them, so don't go obsessing about it. Even though the prices may fluctuate, the dividends will keep coming in.

On the other hand, if you still want to track your stock portfolio, use the Google Finance function in Google Docs to get stock information live. Millions of people track their stock portfolio, and there's no harm in doing it unless you start obsessing over it.

Tracking your dividend portfolio allows you to stay informed about your money, and you will feel satisfied knowing your money is being used to generate profits. You will also be able to know if the stocks you own have decreased in price so you could buy more of them, but cheaper than you did before.

Tracking your portfolio will allow you to re-evaluate your stocks at least once a year. Read up on each company and its metrics to make sure they are all on track and remain a beneficial investment. If their metrics have gone haywire, then you will know it's time to invest in a better, more profitable company.

CHAPTER SIX

Introduction to Financial Freedom

What Do We Know About Financial Freedom?

How frequently do you sit in your work area, wandering off in fantasy land about what would it feel like to put an end to your exhausting nine-to-five employment? Do you have that one companion who is always on an excursion and making every second count and marvel how they pull it off?

Have you, at any point, contemplated selling the entirety of your assets and beginning another life elsewhere? Do you wish you could leave your significant other, but are stuck in the relationship since he's the provider? Do you frequently think about whether you could, in one way or another, transform your stoneware or photography side interest into a genuine business?

If any of these situations sound recognizable, chances are, you lack the freedom to evolve and reach stability financially. Freedom is characterized as the condition of not being detained or oppressed. Now, you may believe you're free since you aren't in jail and don't live in a war zone, yet not attaining financial freedom strips you of a lot of control when it comes to making major life decisions.

As an example, consider your home loan, your vehicle installments, your credit card bills, student loans, and so on. Understudy advances. In case you quit paying those, you'd be sent to collections, your FICO score would dive, and you'd be in financial ruin. Your money related commitments resemble a noose around your neck, and for some, the noose gets tighter as the weight of your budget increases.

That sure doesn't seem like an opportunity. You are most likely committed to numerous money related duties that keep you from reaching your actual potential and accomplish financial freedom.

Financial Freedom is defined as:

"Financial Freedom or independence is the status of having enough money to live without a regular paycheck. In other words, financial freedom is to have enough savings or passive earnings to last you a lifetime without having to actively earn a penny."

There are numerous methodologies to accomplish financial freedom, and each comes with its own set of advantages and disadvantages. To achieve financial independence, you must have a monetary arrangement and a spending plan.

A Closer Look at a Financially Free Life

Financial freedom is about more than just having plenty of money. When you have money in your bank account, attaining financial freedom becomes an opportunity – or for more responsible individuals – a responsibility. Financial freedom allows you the independence to be who you really are and achieve what you want in life. It allows you to take risks, make certain life choices you would never have had you not been financially independent, and ultimately live your life on your own terms.

As many of us set out to fulfill the roles of a parent, spouse, employee, and friend, we lose sight of our financial goals, and our dreams get lost in a whirlwind of compromises. Even though these roles in life are rewarding in their own way, the build-up of underlying resentment due to our inability to achieve our dreams leaves us wondering – what if we'd taken a different route?

To become financially independent, you must let go of the things that hold you back and dedicate your efforts to the achievement of lifetime financial stability. Financial freedom is a process that takes a lot of mental and emotional strength. To achieve your financial goals, you need to become a different person; someone who is more careful with their choices, know what they want, and do not let distractions and hindrances keep them from taking it.

In return, financial freedom will reward you with a powerful, dynamic, and happier version of yourself you didn't even know you could become. And ultimately, achieving your financial goals is your true reward of financial independence.

Importance of Financial Freedom

Financial Freedom is significant because it gives you the power to choose how you decide to spend your life. A great many people think it is inconceivable or challenging to accomplish, and this might be valid. However, as difficult and challenging as it may be, you need to remember that it is not impossible. Reflect on how the choices you have made today will affect your life tomorrow, and you will understand how the minor changes can put you on a path to financial freedom.

- Financial freedom allows us to live life the way we want without having to constantly think of the repercussions or the toll it would take on our bank account.
- You get to enjoy a comfortable life and have the chance to explore new things and have new experiences.
- You have the flexibility to make choices and are independent in control over your money and expenditure.
- You are finally in a position where you no longer have to worry about your own supply of cash and can help others. Moreover, you get more time to spend amongst family and friends.
- Nothing can stop you from giving your lifelong dreams a shot, pursue your goals, and live a happy and fulfilling life.
- For once, you have a clear vision of your objective in life and are not afraid to go after it.
- You learn to enjoy and appreciate what you have in life.

- You become more ambitious, more determined, and aspire to achieve more.
- You have control over how much you work and can live life on your own terms.
- Last of all, you are finally free from financial hassles and have peace of mind.

The above points highlight the importance of financial freedom and how it can help us achieve financial stability for the rest of our lives.

Taking steps to achieve financial freedom may be a difficult task, but with the right motivation, nothing you aspire to do is impossible. Distributing your financial objectives into little steps or levels can help you get on the road to financial freedom while making the procedure more sensible, and ideally, somewhat less unpleasant.

Even if you are starting out by making little changes, the significant thing is to start.

Listed below are the eight different levels of financial freedom to help make your life financially more fulfilling:

Level No. 1 – Stop Living Life from Paycheck to Paycheck

Sadly, living paycheck to paycheck is the reality of countless Americans. According to the 2017 report submitted by the Federal Reserve on the Economic Well-Being of U.S. Nuclear families, some 40% of families were incapable of taking care of a $400 unexpected expense. Most of us have some unexpected bills spring up from time to time, for instance, vehicle fixes, specialist's visit costs, and nights spent drinking with friends. Having some money stashed away will end up being valuable during these circumstances.

Level No. 2 – Have Enough to Resign from the Job

Financial freedom is all about making work a choice rather than an obligation. Having put aside enough money to be able to resign from your job, forever, is an incredible opportunity you create for yourself. Maintaining enough cash influx to have the choice to take some time out from work is a critical step toward financial freedom. It doesn't imply that you have to leave your job, yet it is somewhat satisfying to know you can without having to face a financial crisis.

Level No. 3 – Have Enough Money to Achieve Financial Stability

It is important to earn enough to be financially stable and secure. There is a freeing, independent sensation you get when you realize you are adequately saving, doing the things you love, and still have extra money toward the end of the month.

That extra pad can be used to make the financial climb to independence and stability, given; you keep away from piling on expenses.

Level No. 4 – Have Free Time on Your Hands

What most people need is more flexibility with their timetables. The chance of having the freedom of time and cash related opportunities go inseparable. Together, they are connected to leaving a comparatively sedentary lifestyle to follow your passion, or spend more time enjoying life with your family without having to worry about a draining bank account.

Level No. 5 – Have Enough Money to Cover the Necessities

As a financial planner, I have met a lot of people who absolutely detest going to work. These individuals would probably give a kidney to be able to retire earlier in life. They are willing to go through with all sorts of major changes, even if it means uprooting their entire life just so they wouldn't have to spend hours on a job they hate. The changes may include moving to a country where living costs are comparatively lower, selling their high maintenance home, decreasing living standards, or living with a roommate. Keep in mind that most, if not all, of these individuals were nearing their retirement age.

For such people, it is important to consider if they could really incorporate the kind of changes in their life that early retirement demands. Would they be okay with cutting down on weekend getaways? Can they live in a place that does not cost as much as their current home? If the answer is in the affirmative, it's time they begin working towards a nest egg that will allow them to live this lifestyle.

Considering the minimum living costs after the retirement and knowing you have enough of what it takes to support such a lifestyle will cast a massive impact on your other lifestyle choices.

Level No. 6 – Have Enough Money to Retire Comfortably

Assuming you are doing truly well and are happy with your present way of life, do you have a plan in place to keep up your current standard of living once you retire? You must understand that to collect a retirement fund to support such a lifestyle is a notable achievement. The awards are given to individuals who have done well for themselves, created steady streams of passive income, and are in a position to be able to resign comfortably.

Level No. 7 – Make Enough Money to Have Your Dream Retirement

Imagine not having to spend hours working on a desk job. What would your life look like had you had more time on your hands? Would it involve lots of traveling? Backpacking through Europe with your loved one? Or would it be all about first-class plane rides, staying over at 5-star hotels, and dining in grand style? Let your imagination run free and see where it takes you.

Now given you are making an effort to attain financial freedom, how awesome does it feel to realize you are on track to living your dream lifestyle once you retire? Achieving financial freedom is all about getting there before you're too old.

Level No. 8   Make Enough to Outlast Your Expenses

This level streamlines financial independence to the core. Ideally, your financial independence plan will enable you to outlast your cash. Having more money than you require spending is remarkable. However, having amassed enough wealth to never run out of it is another story. The group of people who are fortunate enough to have this much money are either those who have won lotteries, inherited plenty of wealth, or are founders of top running organizations like Bill Gates, Elon Musk, Jeff Bezos, or Warren Buffet.

These are the people who couldn't possibly outspend their wealth. They could go on a spending spree, give away massive amounts of money, yet they'd still have more than most of us combined.

Now, have a look at your financial circumstances and compare to see where you are on the levels of financial freedom. Constantly motivate yourself to work towards your financial goals, make plans to increase your wealth, establish streams of passive income, and never cease your efforts.

12 Steps to Financial Freedom

Financial freedom is a goal that not many can achieve. It means having enough reserve funds, ventures, and money saved to bear the cost of living for ourselves and our families. In addition to this, we must also have a nest egg that would allow us to retire comfortably or pursue a career we want without being driven to earn a specific sum every year.

However, many of us fail to achieve this. We are troubled by our increasing responsibilities, money related crises, reprobate spending, and all these issues keep us from achieving our financial goals.

Four Basic Pillars of Financial Freedom

Before discussing the step-by-step progression to financial independence, let's shed some light on the pillars of financial freedom listed below:

- **Income Management**

Have a steady stream of income through your active and passive earnings, business, and investments.

- **Debt Management**

You must pay your bad debts as soon as you can and invest your good debts and profitable ventures.

- **Expense Management**

Spend your money wisely and do not pule on expenditures.

- **Asset Management**

Approach low-risk investment strategies and multiply your wealth through incoming profit returns.

Financial Freedom Plan in 12 Steps

Here's a 12 step financial success plan to put you on the road to financial freedom.

1. Set Life Goals and Stay Committed to Your Financial Plan

A general desire for "financial freedom" is extremely ambiguous for an objective. What does it actually mean to be financially independent? What do you see for yourself when you speak of financial freedom?

Note down your bank balance, your expenses according to your living standards, and at what age you aim to achieve complete financial independence. The more specific and direct you become with your goals, the easier it will be for you to achieve them. Now count backward until you reach your current age and check off financial milestones periodically as you go. Now, once you are done, put this sheet of financial goals at the very beginning of your binder to keep reminding yourself of your goals, especially when you face setbacks.

It is extremely important to stay committed to your goals. You must be dedicated to achieving financial freedom despite every curveball thrown your way. Most people start out strongly yet abandon their goals at the first setback. Remember, those who strive, succeed. Those who do not strive will never know what it is like to accomplish something. All things considered, take small steps and avoid making drastic changes to your lifestyle.

2. Create a Budget and Track Your Expense

Create a household budget and stick to it. Plenty of people make a household budget, but more often than not, they end up overspending. Controlling your expenditures and sticking to your budget is the best way to ensure that all the bills are paid on time, you are saving enough, and if you are too good at this, you might even end up with some money to spare by the end of the month. It is important to understand that a month to month schedule fortifies your objectives and reinforces your resolve against the impulse to abandon them.

You must be mindful of your spending and be self-aware to remain on the road to financial freedom successfully.

3. Pay Your Credit Card Bills in Full and Score Quick Financial Wins

Strike off two words from your dictionary: splurge and

loan.

Splurging is what takes you off track when you are well on your way to achieve your financial objectives. But more often than not, money spent splurging can be recovered by increased savings and earnings. However, loans have more of an avalanche effect. They trigger interest that keeps multiplying, and as time passes, it gets increasingly difficult for you to find your way out of the web of interest that swallows all your financial goals.

Think of interest as a wall you keep breaking down, but it keeps building itself back up. And this wall is eventually built high enough to block sight of all your financial goals. This is why it is important to pay off the full balance of your credit cards each month. You do not want interest piling up. Credit card bills and other high-interest loans are toxic to your financial goals. On the other hand, student loans and mortgages do not have high-interest rates, so there's no urgency in paying off those.

4. Create Automatic Savings and Set up a Mini-Emergency Fund

You must pay yourself first. Enroll yourself into an employee retirement plan and benefit from contributions made to your pool of funds. Next, set up an automatic withdrawal to tap into your emergency funds if the need for it arises while simultaneously setting up a contribution to your brokerage account. In an ideal situation, the money that is supposed to go into your brokerage account should be pulled the same day you receive your salary, completely avoiding the chance for it to slide into your checking account.

However, you must realize that the recommended amount to save is not the same for everyone, and you must decide for yourself how much you wish to save and invest.

At this point, you ought to gain considerable ground, and ideally, start seeing some cash leftover from every check. To lessen the danger of abandoning your objectives when you face a setback, you are going to put aside $1,000 and put that into an investment account. The goal is to have this money to assist you with profiting.

5. Begin Investing

Building your wealth by investing is a tried and tested strategy using which millions of people grow their money and generate a stream of passive income. Compound interest – collecting interest on interest – will make your money grow at a faster rate, but you will still need time to achieve a growth that lasts.

Investing can be tricky. So don't start by thinking you're the next Warren Buffet and second guess the movements of the stock market. Open an online brokerage account, learn the basics of investing, create a dividend portfolio, and make automatic monthly contributions to it.

6. Be Mindful of Your Credit Score

Your credit score has more impact on your life than you'd like to think. It determines the rate offered when you purchase a new car or when you are looking to refinance your home. It also affects your car insurance and life insurance premiums. The reason behind this is to check for your credibility and make allowances accordingly. Someone with a dwindling credit score, unstable financial condition, and reckless lifestyle is bound to be into dangerous habits like drunk driving.

This is why it is advised to get a credit report from time to time to make sure there is nothing bad in the records that could potentially mar your financial well-being.

7. Negotiate for Goods and Services

Most American citizens do not negotiate for goods and services they avail because they think it will make you come across as cheap. If you begin negotiating for what you feel is yours, you'd be able to pay thousands of dollars each year.

Maybe large corporations won't pay much heed to what you have to say, but small businesses are susceptible to customer feedback and are usually open to negotiations. When making bulk purchases, you can ask for discounts and save yourself some money.

8. Educate Yourself Continuously

The US government is constantly making changes in tax laws every year. You must keep yourself updated with the latest reforms and changes to make sure you are taking advantage of tax deductions to the maximum. Stay on top of all financial news and the latest trends in the stock market and make adjustments to your investment portfolio accordingly.

There are people out there looking to prey on novice investors who do not have much knowledge about the workings of the stock market. This is why you must learn as much as you can and fight your defense against people looking too prey on new investors and make quick bucks.

9. Provide Maintenance

Maintenance only costs a fraction of what replacement does. This is why it's important that you take proper care of your property from your car, home, and lawnmowers, to your shoes and clothes, etc. When things last longer, you do not need to make replacements very often, which in turn could save you a lot of money.

10. Do Not Try to Match Your Living Standard to Your Income

Most people raise their living standards as soon as they get a well-paying job, a promotion, or make huge profits in their business. An economic lifestyle will not keep you from living your life to the fullest. Mastering a lifestyle where you do not spend as much as you warn is not as difficult as you might imagine. In fact, many wealthy individuals keep their living standards well below the quality they could afford, and they have been in the habit of doing so since well before they became successful and wealthy.

This isn't a challenge to adopt a minimalist lifestyle and dump all your belongings in a dumpster. Steps to financial freedom are all about making small changes and evolving so we could put healthier habits into practice.

11. Hire a Financial Advisor

Once you have gotten to a point where you have built a good amount of wealth, whether they are liquid investments, tangible or intangible assets, you should get a financial advisor to educate you about investment options and help you make well-informed and smart decisions that could propel you on the road to financial freedom.

12. Never Neglect Your Health

Your property is not the only thing that needs maintenance; your body needs proper maintenance, too. At the end of the day, you are focusing all your efforts to attain financial independence for yourself. But what happens when in doing so, you lose sight of the most important asset of yours? Your health.

Make sure you take proper care of your body. Do not overeat or put your body through the wringer very often. It will take its toll on your physical and emotional health. Too much stress will eventually tire you and prove to be detrimental for your health.

CHAPTER SEVEN

Dividend Investing for Financial Freedom

The Ultimate Guide to Achieving Financial Freedom with Dividend Income

What is Financial Freedom?

This is one of the most commonly asked questions, especially when we talk about investing and making future financial plans. It involves planning for the rest of your life in the most reliable and less risky ways.

Basically, financial freedom is to have enough money or to finance your dream lifestyle for the rest of your life without being employed. When you talk about financial independence, you don't consider yourself to be part of a dependent population. Rather, you are earning enough through passive income without being employed.

In short, financial freedom means to earn enough in term of passive income that you can cover all your living expenses and could sustain your living standard, but cutting extra costs and lowering your budgets, eliminating those activities and expenses that you might think are important, but in actual they are less important and are not necessary for your living then ending it would not affect your living.

In this topic, we will focus more on the initial helps that you might need to take when creating a safe and sound future plan to achieve financial freedom. We will keep highlighting dividend income as the most reliable option to achieve financial freedom. After this, I hope you would realize that it is not that difficult to achieve it.

The Road to Financial Freedom through Investment in Dividend Stocks

It is not as easy to achieve financial freedom as it seems, but rather not so difficult too. Today we have reached the time in the history of humans when we are not as stuck in debts as we used to be. But still, we have not been fully successful in becoming free of debts. If any of you have managed to become debt-free, then maybe it's the perfect time for you to think about achieving financial freedom.

You only need to follow the steps mentioned below, and you will be able to give your plan shape of reality.

1. Set Your Goals and Priorities Accordingly

The first step is to determine your goals, and you need to set some priorities as well. This might be the right moment to decide how much you would need to live. For this, you might need to calculate your net worth, by deducting the debts you owe from the assets you own.

Particularly, you are required to prepare and maintain a net worth statement, which actually is a personal balance sheet that shows where your current financial standing. This document should always be there with you throughout the whole financial year to help you determine the progress of achieving financial freedom. And if your net worth starts to decline, then this warning alarm is enough to understand that your whole procedure is not taking you towards financial freedom; rather, it is moving you further away from achieving your objectives and aims that you set earlier.

Many of you question that when the right time to start is. According to most experts, yesterday was the best time to start with this. And the second-best is today. You can immediately start making money by dividend growth investing. For this, the only thing you need is a brokerage investment account either in the stock market or on online cloud computing platforms.

2. Trace and Maintain Your Cash Flow Balance

To achieve financial freedom, you need to keep track of your paid and unpaid expenditures. It will allow you to look into the details related to each year's taxation. Before going into further details, answer a question that does your financial year ends with a positive or negative balance? If it's a positive or a surplus, it means that your business is performing well, and you are not going to face any liquidity crisis anytime soon. But it also provides you with a valid reason to cut extra and unnecessary expenses and to increase the inflow of other incomes. What matters the most is that never ignore any of your invoices, rent, utility bills, or payrolls and keep a regular check and balance on all of them.

The most convenient way to track your net cash flow balance is to keep an eye on the cash balance after the deduction of tax and separate it from the amounts you have paid or surely will pay for the current monthly bills. You will find out that many of those bills are easy to calculate or anticipate, while for the rest of them, you have no other option than relying on the approximated amounts and calculations. Also, do not forget to include such expenditures that only incur a few times each year like gym subscription cost, traveling, etc.

3. Try to Manage Within What You Have and Your Means

Another vital step to take is to cut all the unnecessary costs that you think are not there to improve your living standard. For instance, many people like to dine out with their mates in lavish restaurants and going on expensive vacations. In reality, if they stop doing all these, then hardly there would be an effect on their living, as all these are only their luxuries and not necessities of life.

Hence, excluding them might not create a significant effect on that person's life, but it would emerge as a major reason, leading to a decrease in the required amount you would need for financial freedom.

Therefore, the less your cost of living, the less the amount you would need to save to achieve financial freedom. Moreover, the main purpose is to tell you that this way, you can create a surplus of cash, which later on will assist you in achieving your goals in less time.

4. Draft Yourself an Action Plan

Till you reached this step, you would have learned that

what are your financial standings and have already set your life aims and goals to plan and work accordingly. Moreover, you would also be done by calculating how far you are now from achieving each goal. So now is the right time to start working and show some progress on the road to achieve those objectives.

The simplest way of doing this that I can suggest is by reducing your overall unnecessary spending, try to save more, and invest in multiple investment plans with a higher return. Many of you would complain that it is easy to say, but it gets a lot difficult when you start doing it. So we have drafted the following actionable steps that can make this whole procedure a lot easier.

- Always know the due date for any expense and always remember your outstanding debts to avoid inconvenience.
- If you are in a relationship and any of you only work part-time, then you should prefer doing a full-time job to increase the overall household's income.
- Highlight the possible challenges and hindrance that you might have to face when working towards achieving your goals and also determine tactics and strategies to help you with targeting and working on those objectives.

5. Review Your Taxes Multiple Times

You might already know that reducing the amount of tax levied on your income might also help you with this process. But what you don't know is that when you manage an investment portfolio, it means that your income falls under a completely different tax bracket. And to understand this, you need to look and determine how each bond is different from others, how the dividend income is taxed, and how the tax system treats your capital gains.

Probably, for you, the most suitable solution to this problem is to discuss your queries from a tax professional or a tax consultant, who can advise you accordingly.

6. Determine In Which You Are More Willing To Invest

It is always advisable for new and inexperienced investors to draw up a detailed financial plan, and go according to it. But it should not be crossing the limitations that you are unable to afford it. For all these kinds of plans, there comes an Investment Policy Statement, which is a specified plan for beginners that entails how and when you should spend or invest your money. You are new in the investment market, and this plan would work perfectly for you, allowing you to stick to your objectives and goals, even when the conditions in the market are not stable or are volatile.

Investments plan or policies are drafted, taking some considerations into account. These might include the availability of time and how much and for how long you can tolerate the risk involved. Those investors that have more time available and invest for a long-term goal, also have enough finance for the backup. Hence they are more likely to be generating a bigger part of revenue.

7. Draft a Plan for Yourself

Your plan should be based on the following five different

sections; this way, it would appear like the easiest thing to do:

- Your Latest financial position or situation
- Your primary and secondary financial objectives and goals
- Your statement of net worth
- Steps you would require to reach your final goals.
- The Investment Policy Statement

Using Dividends to Boost Saving Goals for Financial Freedom

In terms of a business or as an investor, you should be setting your priorities of earning more of the passive income rather than active income. It is because time is moving fast and is only limited. You cannot earn more and more active income through a nine-to-five job.

Therefore, you should opt for investing in dividends, for which you don't have to do much and would still receive dividend income regularly. The best thing that I have come across, and you definitely would also be, coming is that investing in dividends helps a lot in boosting the saving and your finance at an increasing rate.

For many, especially those people that are struggling to get ahead financially, the process of financial planning to achieve financial freedom might be the most complicated and challenging task. As, they are planning to quit their jobs to invest, but are confused that the saving they currently have are sufficient or not. They are also confused about the rate of return they would receive on investment and would it be sufficient for their living. And actually, they find the answer to these questions a bit complicated to understand and not the whole process.

We have worked restlessly and tried our best to make and introduce you to an easier way to achieve financial freedom. The first thing you would learn in the upcoming details is about determining the amount you would need to save, to invest at a later date. Moreover, you would also go through the process to boost your savings through dividends and to achieve financial freedom with all the essentials and affordable luxuries of life.

Determine the Amount to Save

The first step you need to take on the road towards financial freedom is to decide or set a minimum goal on how much amount or a percentage of the earning to save. As mentioned before, financial freedom is all about earning or having enough required finance to live a life of your dream or to sustain the desired living standard and getting all that without doing the work.

According to many published pieces of research, a 4 percent rule has been introduced. It states that 4 percent is the safest rate of withdrawal for a wide range of stock or investment portfolio to generate enough long-term and persistent dividends. It means that having 4 percent of dividends out of your stocks is more long-lasting than having a 7 to 8 percent, especially when we are not ready to take a lot of pressure and risk in our later years.

Work toward Your Target Amount

The next and the most vital step is to work towards your

goals and targeted amount passionately. Let's suppose that you have set your target to save up to $1 million, so now you have multiple ways to reach it. First of all, determine the amount you need to save each year by dividing the total years you have planned, and the total amount to save. Assuming that we have 20 years to save the amount of $1 million, then after the calculation, we get to this conclusion that if you save $50,000 every year, then by the end of the 20th year, you would be able to save $1 million.

For many of you, saving the amount of $50,000 each year might not possible, but if you can earn even $3000 each month and can conveniently save $600 out of it, then it's good enough. Try to save as much as possible, and cut off all the unnecessary expenses. If you are young and earning a lower amount, then it is usual and always remember that it will take some time to and much effort to earn more. But the point is that you should be saving at any level of income, as in the long run, this will create a significant compounding effect in the process to achieve financial freedom.

How to Save $1 Million in 20 Years with $4000 Earnings Per Month and Expenses Costing up to $2800

Here we have another possible solution for the low-income earners to achieve the goal of $1 million savings in 20 years' time period. Now people earning and spending a decent amount can also be part of our plan to enable you to live a life free of worries and compromises. Without changing your current lifestyle, you can even save a million dollars through the following scenario;

- Should have $200,000 savings at the start

- Should be earning a minimum of $4000 salary per month
- Necessarily receiving bonus salary for three and a half months
- You maximum expenses should not exceed $2800 each monthly
- Invest 80 percent of your savings with only 4 percent dividends as a return

Referring to the above scenario, if you have calculated along, then you would know that you can save a million dollars in only 19 months. Moreover, earning a salary of a minimum of $4000 per month and spending $2800 out of it and investing it as a 4 percent dividend investment would not be a difficult task for many of you. Rather some of you might be earning even more than this amount and are also able to generate higher dividends, allowing you to reach your target earlier than expected.

I want to remind you once again that when we talk about a $4000 salary each month, we are actually talking about the take-home pay, which is only $3200. Therefore, if you spend $2800 out of $3200, then you might need some extra bonuses and dividends on the investment of $200,000, which was your initial saving amount so that you can still save $22000 each year.

The 10 Commandments of Dividend Investing

To accumulate or build wealth and for a regular stream of passive income, the best strategy you can opt for is to invest in those stocks that pay out persistent and high-yield dividends. It is all about taking higher risks, but do not forget that the return on investment is also quite high and convenient as well.

In fact, there is no rocket science involved in such investments, and you can begin with trading today or even now. For investing, the only thing you need to have is the investment account with sufficient finance, and along with this, you need to have a detailed understanding of some fundamentals and basic rules. Therefore, in this chapter, we are going to discuss the ten basic principles or rules that can guide you towards a successful dividend investing.

1. Never Gets Attracted by the Yield

Dividend yield is seemed to be the most important factor influencing the choice of investors whether to invest or not. It is because the higher the dividend yield, the more chances of better return exist. But never rely on just the numbers, as they can be illusionary. What if the payout level of stocks is not consistent, especially when talking about long-term investment? As a result, sooner or later, those high yield dividends would get dried up.

Higher yields can be eye-catchy, but you should look at other figures as well, such as the history of payouts, the liabilities of the company, and upcoming crises due to the change in monetary policy in the country and an increasing interest rate. For a more stable investment option, you might need to sacrifice a high-yield payout in the short run, but believe me, later, it would turn out to be a more profitable approach.

Therefore, many professionals believe that low-yield

stocks with sustainable payout are more appealing than those with high-yield, but poor payout and inconsistent stock price.

2. Stick With Established Companies

Usually, a stock market operates in cyclical direction, hence the share price, which today has been decreasing, once again would increase. Therefore, whenever you have to choose between multiple dividend stock issuing companies, always prefer the one with transparent and excellent past performance in terms of stock and dividends. It is always recommendable to opt for a firm that has the status of dividend aristocrats.

It is given to those well-established corporations that have been consistently increasing their dividends paid on stocks over the last 25 years period. You might identify such firms by either their wide product portfolio or well-recognizable brands, generating steady cash inflow, and making huge profit margins.

3. Look for Growth Potential

It is like a bit of advice for investors that never jump on the new companies in the market, even if they pay you really a fair amount of dividends. And if you are interested in one, then you should be done with your complete and detailed research. Not only the past returns and current payout are important to look at, but also the future capabilities and potential of the company to increase their dividend amount are vital.

In short, it is the description of growth investing in which investors focus more on the long-term outcome and the possibilities for growth to anticipate its profitability, and not on the price of a stock in the market.

4. Be Mindful of the Payout Ratio

The payout ratio for the dividends paid by a company is one of the most reliable ways of determining how risky the investment might prove to be. This ratio is the summary of the amount paid by the company to its shareholders and the income they can possibly retain.

The reality is that, if the company which you are planning to invest in is paying only a little part of their income as a dividend payout to its investors, then I would suggest you to think once again before purchasing stocks, and this time, please be more cautious in making your final decision. It is because they might be facing a decrease in their income, and as a result, they might also be cutting off the amount of dividend receives.

5. Mix It Up

Many investors would agree with what I am going to say that never invest your all finance in one specific sector of the market. Always try to have stocks from multiple companies and industrial sectors. There is no doubt that the companies and sectors you have opted for might have an extraordinary track record. But have you ever planned for the time when the sector faces a decline during an economic recession?

So if you would have your money circulating in multiple sectors, then it might give you an edge. Creating a wide investment portfolio is a smart choice to make, as this would diversify your investment, allowing you to minimize the risk involved. In the case of downfall in a market, you might be facing losses, but the rest of your portfolio would help in recovering it.

6. Know When to Hold and When to Fold

Like any other smart investor, you should know how long you need to hold the investment to make enough profit. Many investors believe in adopting the long-term approach when investing in dividend stocks, but they also know when and how to cut their losses. The long-term approach means to hold on to your investment until you earn an equivalent return and not hanging on for too long.

It is a common mistake that many new investors make that they get attracted by the face value of the stocks in the market. And later, they face losses when, unfortunately, the company is unable to deliver the expected growth. So, you should have the skill of recognizing that when the share is about to sink, as you have to act accordingly, and when to hold it tightly.

7. Always Reinvest Dividends

If you would ask me to explain how powerful the reinvesting of dividends can be, then I am sorry I have nothing to tell you. But I can show you the performance of many financial institutions that have been generating higher profits through accumulating returns and reinvesting them back in the firms. It is one easy method if you are more interested in making a wide investment portfolio in less time.

Through the use of dividend reinvesting program, you can save more by not paying the amount of commission again and again, as it gets exempted. It works like a loop, and with time, when the payout increases along with it, your capital investment increases, and again you invest it in some other stocks.

However, it is not for those investors who either make a short-term investment or have planned to spend their retirement life depending on the dividend income.

8. Heed the Tax Implications

The tax rates levied on the passive income earned through investing in stocks do not remain the same throughout the year. Lawmakers or the government, in an attempt to make an equitable system, keep on changing the taxation laws applicable to your dividend income. In many countries, where the tax rate on capital gain is less than the rate of income tax, people prefer dividend incomes more than salaries. As an investor, getting yourself into a lower tax bracket allow you to enjoy more of the disposable income than those receiving salaries.

9. Understand Foreign Dividends

The United States stock market might be the largest one in the whole world, but still, it only represents 50 percent of the global investments. Therefore, investors should not only have an understanding of worldwide stock markets but should also keep an eye on stocks in other countries and their regulations as well.

10. Do not Fall in a Value Trap

Have you ever heard of the term value trap? Yes, many simple and profitable looking dividend stocks later have proved to be the worst choice of investors. The value trap is actually a phenomenon, in which due to a fall in price stock seems cheaper with a strong dividend yield. Due to a fall in price, the stock can attract the attention of many investors.

To identify a value trap, you should look out for those firms that are paying higher dividends than their mates in the market. Moreover, those firms with falling cash flow, but are still paying a good and stable return are one of the examples of value trap.

CHAPTER EIGHT

DIVIDEND STOCKS FOR 2020

Top 10 Dividend Stocks – 2020

2020 has only just begun, and the stock market has already experienced a massive uptrend. The unemployment rate is 3.5% - the lowest it has been in the last 50 or so years. Moreover, the American economy is tightening its claws on financial stability and getting stronger by the hour. As investors continue to seek profitable sources for investment, here is a list of the best dividend stocks, you should definitely look into buying this year.

Each of these dividend stocks has the potential for growth and offers promising capital appreciation and yields that are incomparable to the other stocks on the market.

As dividend stocks climb up the monetary ladder, the yields tend to decrease. The yields recorded on the S&P 500 started out at over 2% and closed at 1.8% toward the end of the year. This sets an example as to how the US stock market continues to break its own records and climb new economic heights. However, this makes it all that harder for investors to look for high-profit stocks that offer dividend payouts above the average range.

To provide you with the list of the best 2020 dividend stocks, we have looked high and low at the S&P 500 for stocks offering dividend yields 2% or more. S&P Global Market Intelligence overviews experts' stock appraisals, giving them scores based on their profitability to the investors. It scores them on a five-point order, where 1.0 equivalents Strong Buy and 5.0 means Strong Sell. Any score of 2.0 or lower implies that experts rate the stock a Buy.

Finally, we dove into research and experts' evaluations on the top-scoring names of dividend stocks for 2020. Here's a list of our top 10 picks:

- **JPMorgan Chase**

    Dividend Yield: 2.6%

    JPMorgan Chase & Co. is an American multinational holding company that excels at investment banking and financial services. Headquartered in New York City, JPMorgan is ranked as the largest bank in the United States and the sixth-largest in the world by total asset value of $2.76 trillion (USD). JPMorgan has been paying dividends for 20 consecutive years, with dividend growth of 17% recorded over the span of the past five years.

    Investment in JPMorgan stock yields a dividend income of $3.60 per share annually. On a scale of most stable to most volatile dividend-paying companies, JPMorgan Chase has ranked 7 for the past five consecutive years. This corporate giant has delivered a compound stock market return of 146%

for the same duration. On a scale from 0 to 99, JPMorgan chase is 8 for the earnings stability factor. With a dividend payout ratio of 34.5%, JPMorgan has raised its earnings per share at an impressive 12% for five consecutive years.

- **Home Depot**

    Dividend Yield: 2.47%

    Our next pick is The Home Depot, Inc., which is America's largest home improvement retailer that supplies tools, construction products, and services. The Home Depot is a promising home improvement chain that offers long-term dividend growth. Currently paying its investors $1.36 per share, The Home Depot has shown 20.4% increment in stock value over the past three years. The home improvement company has also raised its per-share earnings at 21.52% over the past three years.

- **Bristol-Myers Squibb**

    Dividend Yield: 2.8%

    Headquartered in New York City, the pharmaceutical giant Bristol-Myers Squibb has already gobbled up Celgene and scored a spot on our list for the best dividend stocks to buy in 2020. As is the case with most pharmaceutical companies, Bristol-Myers Squibb excels through its reach and resources that enable this biotech giant to deliver innovative medicinal drugs for the treatment of life-threatening, fatal diseases.

    Bristol Myers Squibb boasts a strong dividend history with a 2.6% dividend growth rate achieved over the span of the past three years. It currently pays out $0.45 per share to its dividend stock investors, while its earnings have shot off the scales with a three-year growth rate of 166.40%.

- **Nike**

    Dividend Yield: 0.96%

    The American multinational corporation, Nike, Inc. excels in the design, development, manufacturing, and sales of footwear, apparel, and accessories. One of the pioneers in athletic clothing, Nike, is a promising candidate for long-term dividend growth. Its recent three-month performance shows an impressive improvement of 8.43%. Its latest earnings and an impressive dividend growth rate of 11.5% make it one of the best dividend stocks to buy in 2020.

    Headquartered in the metropolis of Portland near Beaverton, Oregon, Nike pays its investors a current per share dividend payout of $0.245.

- **Medifast**

    Dividend Yield: 4%

    We know that the best dividend stocks are those that could offer meaningful dividend yields to their shareholders and promise a sustainable dividend growth rate over time. The US-based nutrition and weight loss company Medifast that sells healthy meals and owns five subsidiaries checks both boxes. As per its dividend payout ratio of 48%, Medifast pays a smidge less than half its earnings to pay its dividend investors. The remaining half it uses to reinvest in the business and finance its growth.

    Medifast is expected to propel its earnings another 20%

annually over the span of the next five years. With a high appreciation potential and an impressive dividend payout ratio, Medifast has well-deservedly scored its place on our list of the best dividend stocks for 2020.

- **Discover Financial Services**

    Dividend Yield: 2.1%

    With Visa, MasterCard, and American Express soaking up the spotlight, Discover Financial Services often fades into the background. An American financial services company, DFS, grows each year steadily. It offers a 2.1% dividend yield to its investors, but according to its annual earnings records, DFS has plenty of room to grow its dividend payout ratio.

    It utilizes only one-fifth of its yearly earnings to pay off its investors and has excellent potential for stock appreciation in the future. All of these factors combined make DFs an excellent prospect or dividend investment in 2020.

- **Texas Instrumentals Incorporated**

    Dividend Yield: 2.8%

    Texas Instrumentals Incorporated or TXN is a leading US-based semiconductor company promising long-term dividend growth. This American technology company specializes in the design, manufacturing, and sales of semiconductors, processors, software, and integrated circuits globally.

    Headquartered in Dallas, Texas, this technology firm exhibits a strong dividend history with a currently paying out $0.90 per share in dividends and a growth rate of 23.4% over the span of the last three years.

- **Merck & Co.**

    Dividend Yield: 2.67%

    Merck & Co, Inc. is an American multinational pharmaceutical company with an impressive dividend history and a recently announced rise in its dividend payouts. For investors seeking to invest in dividend stocks that promise long-term dividend growth, Merck & Co. is an appealing choice. Merck's high demand stock exhibits an excellent growth rate of 3.2% over the past three years. Currently, it is paying its shareholders $0.61 in dividends every quarter of a year.

- **Intel Corp**

    Dividend Yield: 2.1%

    Intel is another leading semiconductor manufacturing company based in Santa Clara, California, in Silicon Valley. A member of the Dow, this semiconductor giant, has been making the US News Best Dividend Stocks list for two consecutive years (2019 and 2020).

    Intel Corp is now looking to focus on data and reinvest in the company to make it more of a data center business, which now makes 33% of its total revenue. With a dividend payout ratio of 29%, Intel Corp has set a four-year straight record of generating the highest revenue at 14 times earnings on capital gains, making it a well-priced dividend-paying corporation.

- **Verizon**

    Dividend Yield: 4.1%

    With a market value of $250.2 billion, Verizon is an American telecom company that specializes in the sales of wireless products and companies. Solely focus to top its own records in the wireless business, Verizon has restructured its business framework to the launch of 5G. While Verizon is hoping to deliver its 5G service to 30 major global telecom markets (10 of which were already launched toward the end of 2019), this year, we should see a substantial process in the stock price of Verizon Wireless.

- **Takeaway**

The corporations mentioned above are all excellent prospects for dividend investment promising tremendous dividend growth rate and stock appreciation. Shares of dividend companies like JPMorgan, Bristol-Myers Squibb, The Home Depot, and Nike present a potential buying opportunity backed by their long-standing dividend growth history.

Altogether, this list of the best 2020 dividend stocks makes for an impressive yield-oriented dividend portfolio, and a steady stream of passive income.

CHAPTER NINE

Value of Dividend Growth Investing

Dividend Growth vs. Dividend Yield

Investors show interest in dividend stocks for one of the two or both reasons:

- Dividend Yield
- Dividend Growth

To understand how dividend yield and growth make a difference in the overall dividend income, we must understand what they mean.

Dividend Yield

The dividend yield of a company is the ratio of its annual dividend payout to its share price. It is represented as a percentage and can be calculated using the following mathematical formula:

Dividend Yield = Annual Dividend / Share Price

Dividend Growth

The dividend growth rate is the annual rate of growth that a particular dividend stock undergoes over a specific period, expressed as a percentage. Dividend growth rate can be mathematically expressed as:

Dividend Growth = Year X Dividend / (Year X - 1 Dividend) – 1

Dividend Yield Stocks vs. Dividend Growth Stocks

A company that pays out in dividends is usually a financially healthy and established business, generating enough profits to return cash to its shareholders. Dividends also force the management team to focus on long-term financial goals and decisions regarding capital allocation.

Once a company declares a dividend, it has to be careful with the profits to avoid making cuts in dividend payouts. A financially stable business can afford dividend growth even when it is going through a weaker phase for a few years. However, when there's a cut in dividend payout, it means that the company's profits are dwindling, and its earnings have weakened. This ultimately leads many investors to dump the shares and invest in other financially stronger prospects.

Investment in Dividend Yielders

It's not always the case that stocks yielding higher dividends come from the healthiest businesses with plenty of capital on hand. Having turned a blind eye to all the other factors and only choosing stocks with the highest dividend yield can result in the purchase of high-risk dividend stocks. These stocks are priced relatively lower than their dividends as a result of financial distress.

However, it does not mean that investing in companies with higher dividends is a bad idea. But when you invest in dividend yielders, you must consider more than just the dividend yield. To determine if a company is capable of paying high dividends for the long-term, focus on stocks of companies that have attained financial stability, and have enough to sustain and raise their dividends.

Investment in Dividend Growers

Companies having stable cash flow for a long period raise their dividend payout. These companies are known as dividend growers. While they may not always give you the highest dividend yield, they do grow at a steady rate toward a better dividend payout. Investors must have reasonable expectations from a dividend growth strategy. Those looking for immediate dividend raise may not be satisfied with the yields of a dividend growth portfolio.

This begs the question: what is the appeal in dividend growers? People looking for financially stable dividend stocks find dividend growers appealing for a variety of reasons. These companies are higher-quality, have a firm financial footing, plenty of cash to invest, and hold up pretty well in down markets. Moreover, these companies also participate in up markets and give excess returns after every full market cycle.

Besides being cash-rich, businesses with dividend growth strategies in place are proof against inflation. They provide reassurance to the investors and allow them to maintain their purchasing power in times of inflation.

Takeaway

Ultimately, dividend yield and dividend growth are only secondary factors that help determine how healthy a company is and deduce its long-term supply of cash available. For many traders, investing in companies destined for growth is an enticing concept. However, most investors look for stocks that give high dividend yields and have a strong and steady history of increment in dividend payouts.

Reasons to Invest in Dividend Growth Stocks

Dividend growth investing is a powerful investment strategy for those who seek to harness the power of the stock market to add to their riches and achieve financial freedom with time.

Listed below are five reasons why you should invest in dividend growth stocks to build long-term wealth and achieve your financial goals. With steady investment in dividend growth stocks, you will be able to provide a growing stream of passive income to fund your financial needs and maintain your purchasing power in times of inflation.

- **Both Stock Price and Dividends Will Likely Increase over Time**

The first appeal of dividend growth investing is the financial stability it offers to its investors. Over the long term, dividend growth stocks steadily appreciate, and annual dividends raise, allowing investors to keep a step ahead of inflation and power through the worst recessions and rough economic waters.

When there's frustration amongst traders and stock

owners in the stock market, investors who have made investments in dividend growth stocks find peace in the knowledge that their dividends stocks will prosper during the worst of market meltdowns. This allows investors to reinvest their dividend income in stocks at lower prices to amass shares and add to their total dividend yield.

- **Double-Digit Percentage Declines Do Not Hurt the Investors**

The stock market is a very volatile place. The fear of the unknown and potential financial loss paralyzes investors into either inaction or making foolish decisions. Many will sell their equities in the down market and then reinvest when the downward pressure is gone. These investors miss out on the growth enjoyed by investors who actually added to depressed shares when the market was experiencing downward pressure.

- **You Could Rely on Your Stock Portfolio for Income**

If you are one of those investors who could rely on their dividends for income, you are pretty lucky. Investment in dividend growth stock means you will see very little change in the amount of money you receive. Now even if there's a downturn in the market and share prices drop, you will not be hurt. A diversified portfolio of a minimum of 20 stocks in at least five sectors will provide most dividend growth investors financial stability through the worst of market turndowns.

- **Dividends Provide Comfort and a Sense of Financial Security**

Dividends provide a safety net to investors and allow them

to make smart decisions during trying times in the market that put even the most seasoned investors to shame. During the recession in 2008, dividend growth investors with a diversified portfolio did not have to sell their investments. However, the stories of doom and gloom coming out at the time had most of the investors selling their non-dividend paying stocks when they should have accumulated more shares.

It is important to realize that no equity is perfect. There is no investment that will not disappoint the investor over the decades-long investing timeline. Dividend growth stocks, however, are capable of standing the test of time better than the other stock investments out there. Investors who made smart decisions and had time, patience, and knowledge working in their favor were rewarded with appreciated stocks and incredible growth in dividend yields, allowing them to multiply their wealth.

The key to increasing your wealth via dividend investments is to begin investing early, never stop, and always stay focused. Sooner or later, your efforts will yield remarkable results.

Some examples of popular dividend growth stocks are 3M, Apple, Intel, Boeing, McDonald's, Nike, and Visa.

CHAPTER TEN

Risks of Dividend Investing

Investors are generally interested in spending money on bonds. This is where a large part of a lot of investors' income comes from. The only, and reasonably important, catch with bonds is that they do not offer a safe high-level stream of income. This compels investors to look for better alternatives.

More often than not, high dividend-paying stocks are the most favorite substitutes for investors. We are talking about stocks, and they primarily fall into two categories.

Preferred stock, and;

Dividend-paying common stock

Among these two, the preferred stock is a safer alternative. It is aimed at by investors who are seeking to generate a fixed revenue on their investment without risking their money. Preferred stock typically is determined when the issue at hand is priced, its value doesn't change, and the holders of the preferred stocks are paid dividends before the common stockholders receive their share of the dividends.

The board of directors usually declares the number of dividends to be paid to the shareholders. Depending on their discretion, they can change the amount of the dividend, or they may not pay any dividend at all.

Before we discuss what high dividend stocks are, let's briefly review the definition of dividends.

What Are Dividends?

A dividend is a share of the profit earned by the company during its financial year of operation. A company is owned by those who hold its shares or stocks of ownership, and they get to receive the share of dividends out of the business' profits.

Whether or not the dividends are to be paid to the members is the discretion of the company's board of directors. As a general practice, the dividends are paid on quarterly, bi-annually, or even on an annual basis.

For a dividend to be paid, it is considered important that a company has successfully passed through its growth stage. As long as there is a genuine need to reinvest the profits earned by the company into its developments, the chance of a dividend payout is little.

A dividend is what attracts the shareholders to a company. As shareholders invest in the business by buying shares, they expect to receive profits on their investment. A dividend is kind of a return on stockholders' investment into the company. It is very important that the directors, who are in charge of looking after a company's day to day affairs and business decisions, ensure that the shareholders are interested in investing in their company. If they lose interest and get bored, this might reduce the stock price of a company leading to a decline in its earning and reputation.

High Dividend Stocks

These are stocks that come with a promise to be treated on preferential grounds. This means that the holders of high dividend stocks get paid on a priority basis as compared to the holders of other types of stocks.

While high dividend stocks might seem like a great idea, they have potential risk factors associated with them. The holders of such stocks are indeed paid a dividend in priority, but it is also the truth that these stocks also run high on risks.

Here are some important risks that arise with high dividend stocks.

Effect on the Total Return

As we have stated already, the dividends are paid from the profits earned by a company. In a different scenario, the money would need to be reinvested, which would adversely impact the equity of shareholders. The holders of high dividend stocks are the ones that suffer the most.

For this reason, the actual price of the stock gets adjusted down at the time ex-dividend is traded. This, in turn, has an overall impact on the total return of the value of a high dividend stock.

The Impact on Taxation

Just like all other forms of income, the dividend is also subject to taxation. There are even scenarios where the dividend-paying entity, a company, and the recipients of the dividend by a company are both taxed. That's because dividends are paid out of the profits of a company, which is basically income for the company, leading to their taxation. In the same manner, when the shareholders receive dividends, it is a form of income for them. This means that the individuals receiving dividends will have to pay taxes.

However, taxation relating to dividend income changes drastically according to the political climate prevalent in a country where the company is operating. If you are interested in buying a high dividend stock, you are advised to consult your accountant before finalizing your investment plans.

If you buy the stocks at a time when new tax laws are underway, it would be riskier to put the investment into purchasing stocks. The better option would be to wait and let the taxation atmosphere clear. This helps you in making the right decision regarding the purchase of the high dividend stocks.

Miscellaneous Drawbacks

Other than the two critical impacts described above, there are also additional risks that you must be considered.

If, for instance, the company's profits are dwindling, you should not want to invest in high dividend stocks. You'd be risking your money if you do that.

Another scenario is when the company is about to be taken over by new management. There is a possibility that the new managers would devise new policies focusing on reinvesting the profits into the company to increase its growth. This means that your dividend will fade away.

Thirdly, you should be aware of the lower credit quality risk if you are investing in a preferred stock, hoping that you'd get a guaranteed dividend. You should always keep in mind that the higher the dividend you are promised in such stocks, the lower will be the reliability.

Conclusion

Let us conclude the discussion by reminding you not to fall for a high-paying dividend scheme as the company offering you this is, in all likelihood, not financially strong enough to make the payment. This means that even if you hold preferred stocks, the company is less likely to pay you.

How to Overcome Risks Associated with Dividend Investing?

Every business idea and setup has an element of risk in it. One never knows for sure if their business is going to succeed. The same is the case with investment in the stock. You should know if you are interested, that the risk is always present on the stock market. You are always exposed to the risk of losing all your precious investment if you make a single wrong decision. The risk, nonetheless, is mostly unpredictable and variable.

What impacts your investment the most? What type of risks is usually there?

There is an entire range of factors that will double the risk involved. The good news is that not everything is beyond your control as some risks are manageable if you proceed with caution. Of course, there are other types of risks that you cannot control, but that doesn't mean that everything is beyond your control and measure.

Even though the risks cannot be ever fully eliminated, there is a fair possibility that you can control the extent to which you get exposed to them. To do that, you need to be aware of the factors that influence the occurrence of risks. By understanding these risk-affecting factors in detail, you can mitigate the possibility of risking your investment. This is how the most seasoned investors reduce the risks of their investment. They study risk-causing factors, and they try to mitigate them so that their investment remains safe and secured.

How to Reduce Risks?

This is the main theme of our article. As we have mentioned in the above, investment is always vulnerable to dozens of risks. Fortunately, a lot of these risks can be contained and controlled. In the following lines, we are going to mention what you can do to make sure that there is a minimum risk factor with your investment.

Here are some of the things you can do to reduce the risk of dividend investing.

Keep an Eye Out for fall in Share Prices

This is a highly likely scenario that is independent of the company's past history of paying dividends. In case this happens, you will be facing the worst situation ever. When the company goes bonkers, you might not even have the chance to sell your shares, leading you into a mess. You should be very cautious about it.

Avoid Inflation As Inflation Can Harm Your Savings

You are advised to keep investing your savings into further stocks. If you don't, you run a risk of losing your capital and a downfall in your purchase power. Remember that inflation continues to happen, and it affects each dollar you have. So you should make sure that your savings don't lose value over time, and for that, keep them invested somewhere!

Controlling Human Error

Human error is the most critical risk factor in any dividend investment portfolio. It arises from a range of situations, and by knowing what these possibilities are, the human error can be reduced to a great extent.

The following are some of the forms in which a human error might occur.

- Lack of knowledge about the market.
- Insufficient analysis and research capability.
- An unsuitable investment strategy that does not match the stated goals.
- Not spending time to study the market and market trends.
- Making an emotional rather than rational decision when buying and/or investing in stocks.
- Investment decisions influenced by panic and fear.

These are some of the most important elements that could lead to human error, thereby resulting in the loss for the investor.

How to Control Human Error?

The most effective way to prevent human error during the dividend investing is by doing your homework thoroughly. By assessing the situation dispassionately and without emotions, you will be able to understand what the ground realities are and then make a decision that allows you to benefit from the situation. Moreover, you shouldn't be in a state of panic. Control your emotions and proceed rationally.

Leave Emotions Out

A theory called 'Efficient Market Hypothesis' is a well-known guide that describes in detail how the mechanics of the stock market operate.

The basic principle of this theory is that investors are and should be rational people who make the fullest use of the available information to make decisions that are logical and help them extract profits. Unfortunately, not everyone investing in the dividend may be deemed as a rational or even logical investor. That's because they make decisions based on whatever their friends and relatives tell them. Instead of studying the market and understand the actual realities, they rely on tips from strangers and news in on the TV. As a result of this emotional haste, they end up wasting their resources and suffer loss.

It is advised that when you are in the process of investing in the stock, you should do a detailed study of the company, its management, and the history of the stock. You should make sure that you have spent time studying the market and understand what risks are involved.

Never Spend All Your Investment on a Single Company

This is arguably the most important element to consider. No matter how promising or reliable a company appears, it is always better NOT to invest all your resources into it. Instead, you should spend the money by investing in multiple companies.

The risk factors are significantly huge in putting all your money into a single company. For example, there is a chance that the company has corrupt or incompetent management, or its competitors have a far stronger standing and coverage of the market. Another critical risk is that the company might eventually lose the investors' favor!

Such risks won't bother you when you have investment spreading across multiple companies. That situation prevents you from suffering a huge loss, and you get to have better control over the investment you are making.

The diversification of the investment will lend you credible support in reducing the risks on your investment.

Takeaway

As an investor, you are supposed to be mindful of factors affecting your investment. In the above, we have given you some scenarios that pose a threat to your money. By ensuring to avoid them, you can rest assured that your investment is in safe hands.

CHAPTER 11

TOP 10 ROOKIE MISTAKES TO AVOID

These are ten of the commonest and the most serious rookie mistakes to make with dividend investing. Avoid these and remove some of the risks:

1. Purchasing on Hot Tips

Hot tips are just tips; an idea. You must still research the stock, and that means studying at least a year's worth of quarterly statements for the company. You need to do the number-crunching, look at whether shares are being bought by insiders, maybe even speak to a company rep to see what the company prospects are.

2. Not Doing Your Homework

Those who stand a better chance of winning are those who do the homework, keeping a cool head while all around lose theirs. The best way of doing that is knowing exactly what you own. Then you need to know what you are buying, selling, and why. If you own stocks in companies that have a great track record for sales and profits, not to mention paying dividends, you won't spook quite so much when the market drops suddenly.

3. Buying and Selling Only for Dividends

It would be amazing if we could purchase stocks just before dividends are due for payout, collect the payment and then sell. It might seem like a good strategy for beating the market, but it doesn't work. You may get the dividend payout but, when you come to sell, you'll find the share price has dropped. This is to reflect the payout, sell immediately, and all you will do is break even.

4. Only Focusing on Yield

Most people move from dividend stocks to high-yield stocks, but these stocks can sometimes be an indicator of trouble and not good profit. Yield should not be your focus for determining company growth; sometimes, the companies with lower dividends show stronger growth and consistent rises in dividends, making them a better choice. You need to know why a company has a high yield – is it because dividends are high, their share price is low, or both? Do your homework and ensure you are investing in a sound company.

5. Ignoring Future Dividends in Favor of Current Ones

When looking at dividends for any stock, you see the current one – that's old news. Yes, it's what you get this year, but you're investing, and that means you want to know what the future potential is. We can't see ahead, and we have no way of knowing what a dividend will be but you can look at the following to make an educated guess:

- Recent trends and long-term trends in the company for raising dividends
- Management projections for income

- Important developments that may affect their past trends.

You might be better investing in companies with lower dividends if they show good potential for raising the payout in the future, rather than putting your money into a stock whose dividend is stagnating.

6. Not Monitoring Your Stocks and the Market

Assuming that you put your money onto larger companies with a good track record in paying out dividends, you could sleep a bit better than many speculators or growth investors. You could, but history has shown all too often how big companies can fall at the drop of a hat. Chrysler and Lehman Brothers are two good examples.

You must always monitor your money, keep an eye on your stocks, and watch the news. Listen carefully, and you will often pick up on signs of bad news before things go badly wrong. When you start to hear the experts mention impending bubbles, it's a sign that you need to start paying attention and make plans to get out.

7. Buying Stocks Because They are Cheap

There is a world of difference between low prices and good value, and it's difference between profit and loss. Cheap stocks aren't always a good bargain, and buying cheap stocks is speculating, not investing.

Do your homework on the company fundamentals for cheap stocks. Unlike the bigger stocks, you won't often find very much information about these companies. Where a company can show a good history of dividend payouts, you will rarely find cheap stock prices, but when they do drop, jump at it straight away. Stick to your dividend investment model, and you shouldn't fall foul of temptation to buy a stock solely on a low price.

8. Hanging On To Poor Performers Too Long

It is hard to let go, especially when the stock has performed well previously. It's even tough when you have a stock that has occasional highs that don't last long. Hanging on to sell just to break even is not a winning strategy. Emotional attachments are not wise when you are investing money, and hope is the worst enemy you can have. If a company has had a bad setback and its market share is sliding, never let your emotions stand in the way – sell now, cut your losses and put your money elsewhere.

9. Not Accounting for Taxes

Far too many investors only look at the money they will gain, forgetting to account for the large chunk that taxes can reduce it by. Being successful isn't always about the amount you earn; it's how much of you can keep.

No matter where you invest, you must always take taxes into account. If you gain $200,000 and then lose 35% of it in taxes, you still have $130,000. If your taxes are only 15%, you get to keep 31% more of your money – around $170,000. Do talk to an accountant to draw up a strategy for maximizing returns after tax. And if the government suddenly decides taxes are going up to 30%, make sure you can change your strategy to meet that rise.

10. Paying Too Much Attention to Media Analysis and Reports

Financial publications, investment TV, even financial websites are great places to get good information, but it doesn't mean their info is always correct. They are reliant on company insider information, and if there is one lesson we should learn from the 2008 financial meltdown, it's that management doesn't always let on what's happening and that people do lie.

Never assume that one source is reliable 100% of the time. The best way to get information is to study the financial documents for the company you are interested in. Websites and papers are second, but they make mistakes too. Verify any information you read or hear by looking at other sources and using your own gut instinct.

Conclusion

The next step is to implement the dividend investing strategies you have learned about and buy your first dividend stock. Dividend investors are all about earning steady cash flow from their investments to set them up for life and help them attain financial freedom.

Dividend stocks pay you a small cash dividend per share every four months. Sometimes, dividend-paying companies also roll out dividend income on a one-time basis, as Microsoft did back in 2004. When looking to invest in dividend stocks, look for dividends with a history of steady dividends. You want to avoid dividend cutting at all costs, which is why you must look for dividends that come from cash-rich companies with a history of raising dividends.

Before we conclude, here's everything you have learned summed up as Warren Buffet's golden rules for you to follow:

Always Go for Long Term Value Investing Strategies

Don't let fears or the volatility of the stock market divest you of your best-learned dividend investing strategies. Never sell in a fit of panic and always plan long-term with your dividend stocks.

Do Not Invest in What You Do Not Understand

As per Warren Buffet's investing rules, the simplest one is to avoid investment in anything that is beyond the understanding of a child. Invest in companies that you know will hold up well for the next decade or more.

Buy As If You Are Purchasing the Entire Company

Investment should not be treated as a closed loop of gains and losses. When you purchase stock in a company, always look at its Enterprise Value – the price of the company if you were to buy the whole stock.

Choose Companies with Competitive Advantages

Companies that have pricing power and strategic assets tend to outperform their competition. These companies have enough substance and cash to hold up well during trying times. A good long-term investment strategy involves buying stocks in companies that can weather the good and the bad, both.

Quality Investing is Key to Financial Freedom

Buffet believes paying a fair price for a company that promises growth and increment in dividend yield is better than paying low for a company that will collapse under pressure.

Always Have Cash on Hand

The stock market works in mysterious ways. There's no telling when an opportunity for trade will arise. This is why it is important to have cash on hand to invest whenever an opportunity for it arises.

Purchase Stocks with a Safety Margin

Purchase stocks that have a margin of safety below their intrinsic value. This reduces the risk and allows for adjustments during challenging times.

Dividend Growth Compounding

Long term value investing requires investors to be patient because they grow exponentially. Buffet believes companies that generate sustainable profits have the margin to grow and pay their dividends. Dividend growth compounding multiplies the benefits of exponential growth, and there are not many dividend investing strategies that could top this one.

Equipped with the knowledge you gained from The Beginners Guide to Create Passive Income and Achieve Financial Freedom with Stocks, you are now ready to dabble with dividend stocks. The simplest way is to follow Warren Buffet's dividend strategy: ***buy and hold with a dividend growth stock.***

At the same time, you must keep an eye out for dividend yields that are too high. Often times when this happens, it's a sign that the investors expect the share price to fall in the months to follow. Consequently, any dividend stock with a payout of more than 10% calls for skepticism.

References

1. https://www.investopedia.com/articles/basics/11/due-dilligence-on-dividends.asp

2. https://www.thebalance.com/what-is-dividend-investing-357437

3. http://www.arborinvestmentplanner.com/warren-buffett-strategy-long-term-value-investing/

4. https://www.nerdwallet.com/blog/investing/how-to-invest-dividend-stocks/

5. https://www.thebalance.com/the-ultimate-guide-to-dividends-and-dividend-investing-357453

6. https://lifehacker.com/how-can-i-get-started-investing-in-the-stock-market-1376782232

7. https://www.suredividend.com/pros-cons-dividend-investing/

8. https://www.investopedia.com/ask/answers/090415/dividend-income-taxable.asp

9. https://www.physicianonfire.com/paynotax/

10. https://www.thebalance.com/how-to-pay-no-taxes-on-your-dividends-or-capital-gains-357399

11. https://kclau.com/wealth-management/3-types-of-income-active-portfolio-and-passive-income/

12. https://nataliebacon.com/different-types-of-income/

13. https://myworkfromhomemoney.com/types-of-income/

14. https://www.goodfinancialcents.com/passive-income-ideas/

15. http://escapingtofreedom.com/wp-content/uploads/2017/10/5-Steps-to-Passive-Income-with-Dividend-Investing.pdf

16. https://www.forbes.com/sites/davidrae/2019/04/09/levels-of-financial-freedom/#7570ec7f3860

17. https://www.youtube.com/watch?v=oM_qBYEY80g

18. https://www.investopedia.com/articles/personal-finance/112015/these-10-habits-will-help-you-reach-financial-freedom.asp

19. https://www.youtube.com/watch?v=-ElUilM3k7A&list=PLRwxirm9RENBddr0hyZat0HgKj3pIIlgyY&index=199

20. http://sgyounginvestment.blogspot.com/2019/10/using-dividends-to-boost-savings-goals.html

21. https://www.dividend.com/dividend-education/the-ten-commandments-of-dividend-investing/

22. https://www.investopedia.com/articles/investing/122315/6-rules-successful-dividend-investing.asp

23. https://www.kiplinger.com/slideshow/investing/T018-S001-pros-picks-the-13-best-dividend-stocks-for-2020/index.html

24. https://www.investopedia.com/best-dividend-stocks-4774650

25. https://www.investors.com/research/best-dividend-stocks/

26. https://money.usnews.com/investing/dividends/slideshows/best-dividend-stocks-to-buy-this-year?slide=18

27. https://thecollegeinvestor.com/32466/dividend-growth-investing/

28. https://www.morningstar.com/articles/855088/whats-the-difference-between-dividend-yield-and-dividend-growth-stocks

29. https://www.youngprofessionalinvestor.com/popular-articles/4-reasons-to-invest-in-dividend-growth-stocks/

30. https://finance.zacks.com/dangers-buying-highdividend-stocks-1419.html

31. https://www.investopedia.com/articles/investing/071715/risks-chasing-high-dividend-stocks.asp

32. https://www.dividendmantra.com/2016/02/financial-freedom/

33. https://www.dummies.com/personal-finance/investing/stocks-trading/dividend-investing-how-to-manage-risk-factors-you-can-control/

ETF INVESTING

*The Beginner's Guide to Create Passive Income and
Achieve Financial Freedom with ETF*

BY
HENRY COOPER

© **Copyright 2019 by Henry Cooper - All rights reserved.**

This document is geared towards providing exact and reliable information in regards to the topic and issue covered. The publication is sold with the idea that the publisher is not required to render accounting, officially permitted, or otherwise, qualified services. If advice is necessary, legal or professional, a practiced individual in the profession should be ordered.

From a Declaration of Principles which was accepted and approved equally by a Committee of the American Bar Association and a Committee of Publishers and Associations.

In no way is it legal to reproduce, duplicate, or transmit any part of this document in either electronic means or in printed format. Recording of this publication is strictly prohibited and any storage of this document is not allowed unless with written permission from the publisher. All rights reserved.

The information provided herein is stated to be truthful and consistent, in that any liability, in terms of inattention or otherwise, by any usage or abuse of any policies, processes, or directions contained within is the solitary and utter responsibility of the recipient reader. Under no circumstances will any legal responsibility or blame be held against the publisher for any reparation, damages, or monetary loss due to the information herein, either directly or indirectly.

Respective authors own all copyrights not held by the publisher.

The information herein is offered for informational purposes solely, and is universal as so. The presentation of the information is without contract or any type of guarantee assurance.

The trademarks that are used are without any consent, and the publication of the trademark is without permission or backing by the trademark owner. All trademarks and brands within this book are for clarifying purposes only and are owned by the owners themselves, not affiliated with this document.

THANKS YOU

Before you start, I just wanted to say thank you for purchasing my book.

You could have picked from thousands of other books on the same topic but you took a chance and chose this one.

So, a HUGE thanks to you for getting this book.

Now I wanted to ask you for a small favor. Could you please consider posting a review on the platform? Reviews are one of the easiest ways to support the work of independent authors.

This feedback will help me continue to make the type of books that will help you get the results you want.

Follow the link to leave a review or go on your account.

https://www.amazon.com/review/create-review?

INTRODUCTION

There is no lack of investment ideas out there. Seriously. If we were to sit down and go over every fancy new strategy or product for investing in, we'd probably grow old, die, and then become fossils before we even got halfway through them all! There are way too many choices and it has become simply so overwhelming that you just might find yourself craving the comfort of a good old-fashioned piggy bank that you can break into at the end of the year, or something just as simple. That said though, there is some gold to be found in the dunghill, and that gold is what this book will be exploring. Of course, it's not actual gold, but I dare say it is close enough! What is it? The love child of stocks and index mutual funds. In plain English, I'm talking about Exchange Traded Funds, which you may have heard of as ETFs.

As with anything new and revolutionary, in the beginning, ETFs were just for the big boys. The sharks. The players at institutional levels. Now, though, it's become something you and I as regular people can get into with ease. You don't have to be an investment banker with a $30,000 Rolex and a bajillion dollars sitting in some Swiss account to play. You don't have to be a hedge fund, or own an insurance firm before you can get involved. ETFs used to be just for these sorts of people, because they had more than enough resources to have fun moving Donald Trump sizes of money about. That's great for them, but it also meant that people like you and me couldn't get in on the action. To these firms and big players, $1,000,000 is nothing more than a millionth of a drop in a bucket. For most people, that's life changing money. However, over time I have also got some skin in the ETF game, and I've roped in an impressive number of clients who follow in my footsteps — and it's been profitable.

Ever since ETFs came to be, and right up until now, they have continued to grow in leaps and bounds. I am of the opinion that this growth will keep on going. Now, I'm not about to tell you that the strategies I have and my personal stake in ETFs are solely responsible for the wildly impressive growth of the market, which is currently worth trillions of dollars, but I can tell you with pride and joy that I am a part of this market. The whole point behind writing this book is to get you to see just how profitable this can be for you too. If I do my job right, by the end of this book, you will do the smart thing; you are going to get involved in the ETF market as well, and you're going to win enough to make a difference in your life.

There's a reason you got this book. You want money, but more than that, what you want is security. So, I only have one small thing to ask of you. You may even think of it as doing your own self a favor. Make sure you do not just skim through this. You bought this book for a reason. It's an investment, and the only way it's going to give to you is if you read through it thoroughly, and then put in the work. When you're through with this book, take action! Just as important as taking action is, don't stop learning. Let's dive in!

CHAPTER ONE

Understanding ETFs

The wonderful thing about ETFs is that they have continued to grow ever since they first showed up early in the '90s. You've got thousands of ETFs which you can invest in today, and more than any other product available for investment, ETFS have grown faster. Thanks to ETFs, you, as an ordinary Jane or Joe, can invest without having to pay hefty commission fees, or other hidden fees that you don't understand. These hidden fees and commissions can burn entire black holes in your pockets and bank accounts, pulling a disappearing trick with your money that even the great Houdini could never hope to match or fathom. As if that weren't enough reason to invest in ETFs, it so happens that you can save exponentially on taxes when you invest!

What Is An ETF

Before I get into this, I want you to realize how risky it is to rely on stocks for your retirement. I don't care how seemingly solid a stock tip is, the fact remains that it's risky business. You could invest in individual bonds, but as with any investment, there are risks to consider as well. To make profit from stocks and bonds, most traders and investors work on the principle of "the more the merrier." To play this principle the smart way, you should definitely get involved in ETFs.

An exchange-traded fund or ETF is a security made up of a bunch of securities like stocks, based on a common index. You should keep in mind that ETFs can involve a variety of industries and strategies. They are kind of like mutual funds, except that unlike mutual funds, ETFs can be traded like stocks.

Think of a share of an ETF like a title deed to a house. If you need to prove you own a house, then you've got the deed for the house to help you do that. In the same way, if you've got a piece of a company, then you possess a share which demonstrates that officially. With ETFs, when you own a share of one, that means you've got ownership in a collection of company stocks.

If you want to buy ETFs, or you'd like to sell the ones you've already got, then you've got to do this with a broker. Brokers are like middlemen who connect the ETF market with the rest of us. These days, a lot of these transactions take place online. Back then, this would happen over the phone.

Over the course of a trading day — which in New York time lasts from 9:30 a.m. to 4:00 p.m. — prices of ETFs will fluctuate in line with demand and supply of the securities contained in the ETF.

What an ETF Portfolio Looks Like

At first, the whole point behind ETFs was for them to

follow the price action in a variety of indexes. There's the PowerShares QQQ Trust Series 1 with the ticker symbol QQQ. It used to be called the NASDAQ-100 Trust Series 1, and it currently mirrors the NASDAQ-1000 index's 100 stocks. There's the SPDR S&P 500, with the ticker symbol SPY. This ETF is a mirror of the Standard & Poor's 500, which is basically an index of the United States' 500 top companies. There's also the DIAMONDS Trust Series 1 with the ticker symbol DIA. This serves as a mirror for the Dow Jones Industrial Average index's 30 underlying stocks.

In the portfolio of an ETF, you'll find companies that stand in for a particular market segment or index, like small growth stocks, micro-cap stocks, or the larger US value stocks.

The stock market can be split up into various industry sectors, like industrials, technology, as well as consumer discretionary. For each of these sectors, there are ETFs that represent them. It doesn't matter what securities are represented by your ETF, and it also doesn't matter which of these indexes your securities are tied to. The profit you'll be making from your ETF is connected directly or leveraged to whatever price the underlying securities are valued at. In other words, if there is a bullish or upward movement in the price of gold bullion, or US Treasury bonds, or Medifast stock, then your ETF's value will go up as well. If these prices take a tumble, then your portfolio won't look as pretty.

You can engage in leverage with your ETF. The advantage of leverage is that if the underlying securities in your portfolio were to make a bullish climb, then you would reap two, or three times more profit than you would without leverage. Do keep in mind though, that the rule still applies in the opposite direction. If those underlying securities suddenly turn bearish, then there goes your profit. You may know of leverage, but have you heard of reverse leverage? That is another thing that I love about ETFs. You can make use of reverse leverage, which basically means you can make money even if your portfolios underlying security takes a bearish plunge in value. This of course also means you'll be losing money if the underlying security were to go up in value. The whole point is that ETFs allow you more flexibility, so that with the right knowledge, you can make sure you stay mostly on the winning side of your trades.

Classic Indexes versus New Indexes

You'll find that some ETF providers have a preference for the more traditional indexes. There are others though, who create their own indexes as well. Let's assume you want to buy 1000 shares of the Vanguard S&P 500 ETF. What you'd be purchasing is a part of the traditional index, which is comprised of the big US growth companies. For simplicity's sake, let's assume that the cost of each share is $100. So, you'd have to put down $100,000, and you'd get a stock portfolio which would include shares of companies such as Walt Disney, Netflix, Amazon, Microsoft Corp, and Alphabet Inc, among others. A good ETF provider will give you transparency, so you can figure out exactly what percentage of each company you have. Going forward, I'll be using nice round figures, so that we can keep the math easy to understand. To get the actual figures, you can Google them, or check out the website or feed of your preferred ETF broker.

Some ETFs will also be made up of the companies which are part of foreign indexes. Say you wanted to purchase 1000 shares of the iShares MSCI Japan Index Fund (EWJ), and the market value of the fund is at $5 per share. With $5000, you would have your very own share in the largest of Japanese companies like Mitsubishi, Toyota Motor, and Softbank Corp, among others. Just keep in mind that the S&P 500 Growth Index is mirrored by the IVW, and that the MSCI Japan Index is mirrored by the EWJ.

Let us assume you were to buy 1000 PowerShare Dynamic Large Cap Growth Portfolio shares. That would mean you'd be buying into a **new** index, and not the traditional, classic sort. This ETF you'd be buying is one which has been custom-made by Invesco. There are also other more recent EFTs which are not connected to any index, but are managed. I am of the opinion that it would be prudent to invest following indexes, rather than take part in active investing. However, I do know more than a few clients who have made significant profits from investing actively.

Yet another brand of EFTs is the kind that is used to represent asset holdings besides stocks. You'll find that these mostly represent commodities like gold, oil, and silver among others, as well as bonds. You've also got Exchange Traded Notes or ETNs, with which you can look into other investments like currency futures.

There is some controversy surrounding the new indexes in the ETF world, about whether or not they are worth investing in at all. You'll find that most people have a healthy dose of skepticism when it comes to new things, and these new indexes are no exception. This is not without good reason. It is not necessary for fear of risk, since there is no venture without inherent risk, but because there have been way too many novel investment products and ideas which seemed promising, but have only caused chaos and destruction. That said, it does not hurt to keep one's mind open to potential opportunities to make some profit.

CHAPTER TWO

Why ETFs?

Singles Or A Basket?

Some people are of the opinion that it is better to adopt a "one shot, one kill" mentality, when it comes to investing. However, the saying "do not put all your eggs in one basket" does have its merit, as cliché as it is now. Investing in a variety of stocks instead of just the one will make it easy for you to rest, knowing that your risk is spread out, and you're more protected against sudden movements against your position in the market.

Anything could happen overnight, which could cause a rapid-fire reaction in the value of underlying securities. For instance, some CEO could have been accused of being involved in sponsoring some faction that is working against the United States government. That would be treason. No one wants to be associated with that. Those who are not so bothered by such things would be concerned with the fact that there are those who **are** bothered, who **will** sell their shares instantly. As a result, most shareholders begin shorting their shares, and the value of the stuck plummets to its death, leaving those who weren't so quick on the draw to lose millions, or billions, even. These sorts of occurrences are the norm when it comes to trading stocks. News comes out about something related to the company, the product, the service, or the CEO, and next thing you know, the stock has gone up 300%, or gone down 52%.

When you look at the stock market as a cohesive whole, instead of just a single, solitary stock, you'll find that more often than not, everything maintains an even keel. Everything remains so constant that a dip or rise of as little as 2 percent is considered big news. This is why it makes sense to go with ETFs. With ETFs, you have the perfect means to diversify your investments, for good payoffs in the long run.

Why Invest in ETFs

- They're the smart way to go. The last thing you want is to go for individual stocks. You might as well go to Vegas and blow your money there, rather than try to hit a home run with individual stocks that could plummet and lose you your money on a whim.
- They're the cheaper way to go. Every year, the most you'll have to pay for management is about 0.20 percent. Sometimes, that percentage is even lower. When it comes to mutual funds, however, you'll be charged as high as 1.25 percent annually. It may not seem like a lot, but it does put a dent in your profit as time goes by.
- You'll pay very little in taxes on your profits, thanks to the smart structure of ETFs.
- ETFs offer you transparency. You can clearly see all holdings in your ETF portfolio. You would know at a

glance what percentage of your money is invested in which company. This is way better than mutual funds. Your mutual fund manager is not going to let you see what tricks she's got up her sleeves.

EFTs versus Mutual Funds

At this point, you're probably wondering what difference there is between mutual funds and EFTs, and whether or not you should just stick to your mutual fund manager. While both of these funds deal with baskets of bonds and stocks, they are not the same.

The thing about mutual funds is that while you can place your orders in the day, the real trade will not happen until the close of market. However, with ETFs, you can buy and sell them just like you would buy and sell stocks, and you can actually see the prices fluctuating throughout the day.

Yet another thing about mutual funds is that they are actively managed. ETFs are representative of various segments of the markets, and for the most part, you won't find your ETF manager doing much trading, since it's all managed passively.

When it comes to mutual funds, you'll find yourself having to pay ridiculously exorbitant fees for entering and exiting trades. When it comes to ETFs, if you do pay any fees at all, you'll find that those fees are way, way below what you would be charged by your mutual fund manager.

Thanks to the smart structuring of ETFs, as well as the low turnover in portfolio, there's way less to declare when it comes to taxing your gains, compared to mutual funds.

Big Sharks in the ETF Sea

In the beginning, only the big sharks with the big monies swam in the big ETF Sea. There was a reason for that. Before ETFs became a thing, it was really difficult to place large orders with huge lot sizes all at once. Thanks to the fact that ETFs can be traded during and after market hours, this problem was solved. Yet another thing that the big boys love about ETFs is that they offer a chance for money to be grown or used productively.

Yet another thing that the big players love about ETFs is that you can place market orders, stop loss orders, or limit orders. This way, they can limit their risk with every order, and they know exactly what price their orders will be filled at. This is not something you can obtain with a mutual fund, since orders are only placed upon market close.

Something else that's wonderful about ETFs is the fact that you can make money in both bull **and** bear markets. So, if someone tweets something they shouldn't have, and that instantly sends the price of a stock down to the depths of sheol, then you can simply sell and make money from the plunge, with the intent to buy at a lower price later. This way, your portfolio remains healthy. This is why a lot of hedge fund managers love ETFs.

Little Fish in the ETF Sea

It's not just the big players who love ETFs. The little ones are started to get involved too, at an ever-increasing rate. A lot of people find it hard to believe that they can get involved in ETFs, without having to pay as much as they have had to with other financial products. There are lots of things which new individual players love about ETFs, and low costs are a huge bonus. The average mutual funds charge 1.25 percent of your account balance; however, there are even greedier ones that charge as much as 10 percent!

The sad part is that this does not necessarily mean you will make that money back in the long run. More often than not, you don't, and if you do, you still have to pay commissions and fees for exiting, which can be as high as 9%. So, what's the point? Yet, there are those who'll get into mutual funds knowing this, anyway. The studies have shown that in the end, index funds not only do much better than mutual funds, but also charge way less in expenses, as low as 0.10 percent. Sometimes even lower. This is because ETFs happen to have fewer expenses. With ETFs, everything is processed through a brokerage house, which handles all bookkeeping on your trades, as well as all inquiries. With a mutual fund, they've got to have a mailroom, phone operators, bookkeepers, and stuff like that. Your ETF provider can exist almost entirely in the cloud, and this makes things cheaper. At most, all they have to do is pay a fee to the index creators, but that is negligible.

One more thing to love is that you don't have to hand over your hard-earned money from trading at the end of the year to the government. Most people think the only way to avoid this is by having a tax-exempt retirement account. Back then, before ETFs, you'd have to pay taxes only when you actually had profits when dealing with individual securities. This is not the case with mutual funds, where you have to pay taxes, whether or not you actually turned a profit since you purchased them. With EFTs now, you don't have to deal with this any longer, since there's not much in turnover to give you gains.

The Market Makers

Market makers are the ones who are responsible for creating ETF shares. For every ETF share, you've got a selection of stocks as part of your portfolio. The more your ETF grows, the more shares you have. Each day, you will have fresh, new stocks piled onto the portfolio.

When a seller shorts their ETF shares, the market maker's job is to buy them, and then offer them for sale to a new ETF investor. Let's compare that with mutual funds. If someone were to sell their mutual funds off, then the mutual fund has no choice but to sell off the underlying stock shares, so that the shareholder can be paid off. In the case where the stocks are sold for a profit, then the shareholders have to pay tax on capital gains. Give this enough time, and you'll find that this becomes very expensive.

The good thing is you don't have to worry about this with Exchange Traded Funds, since they are tied to indexes, and index funds do not trade so frequently. For this reason, as well as the structure of ETF funds, as an ETF investor, you do not ever get taxed for your capital gains. This does not necessarily mean you'll never be taxed on them, but if you are, they won't be significant.

It's not quite the same thing that actively managed ETFs, though. Those are not quite as exempt from huge taxes as the regular, index ETFs, but even they are a lot better than mutual funds when it comes to taxes. The long and short of all this is that ETFS are tax-efficient, more so than other financial products. This does not mean you'll never pay tax. You will pay tax on the dividends which your stock ETFs issue, but you won't have to worry about your capital gains being taxed.

Something that is important to note is that if you've got ETFs that are invested in proper commodities, meaning actual gold and silver, you'll be taxed at the rate of 28 percent. If our ETF is invested in taxable bonds, and if it so happens that the taxable bond interests are thrown off, then chances are they will not be as tax-efficient as mutual funds based on taxable-bond. Keep in mind that if your ETF happens to be based on such derivatives as commodity futures and currencies, then you might find the taxes to be complicated, and costly as well. If you've got an account that gives you tax advantages, then you should not have any problems with taxes on earnings from currency swaps, interest, or dividends.

Diversify to Succeed

If you want to actually make a killing from ETFs, then you must absolutely diversify. This is just as important as avoiding unnecessarily high costs like with mutual funds, and improving tax efficiency. The thing is if you're going to diversify, then it is absolutely imperative for you to know exactly what the underlying securities are in your portfolio. The last thing you want is to learn that the funds you've been investing in are all in a particular industry that has been badly rocked by negative news. What this would spell for your investments is doom. So, you must know what you're investing in, and you must make sure it's all diversified.

This is the trouble with mutual funds: You have no idea where your money is going, and your manager will not tell you. You have no idea what instruments your money is invested in. Sometimes it's invested in stuff you wouldn't even touch with a ten-foot pole! Also, there's a study that was done by the Association of Investment Management that showed that a whopping 40 percent of those mutual funds which are actively managed are not quite as they seem. Some of them are aggressive when they seem conservative, and vice versa. Others flip flop between both management styles. The conclusion to draw from here is that you really cannot tell what's up with your money, where it is, or even if it will still be there the next day! What is the fix then? ETFs.

With ETFs, you will have one hundred percent transparency, since you know exactly what it is you'll be buying and always listen on the website of the ETF provider, or their prospectus. You can also take a look on third party financial websites with nothing to gain from misleading you, such as Yahoo! Finance. Just hop on there and type in the ticker symbol, and you should see what all your holdings are in an instant.

Thanks to how transparent ETFs are, it makes it incredibly difficult for your ETF provider to lie about you. An alarming number of scandals have affected the world of mutual funds since its inception, however, ETFs have remained solid. It's incredibly difficult for your ETF manager to manipulate you, since whatever he picks, all of it is connected to an index, which is traded day in and day out, with the price being displayed across hundreds of thousands of computers all over the world. This way, there's no way you could be swindled on account of the price being stale, which happens a lot in mutual funds.

Go for Pro

When you're seeking investment advice, please, go for the actual professionals, not the guy who's making your hotdog, or your colleague from two cubicles over who heard from his cousin Gary about how BootyCoin is the new Bitcoin and will take over the world. Go for the women and men who happen to manage huge foundations, pension funds, and endowments; those who have at least $1 billion in assets invested, if not more. If you keep taking advice from just anyone, what you'll find is you keep buying tops and selling bottoms.

Here's something that's going to blow you away: You can be a professional manager, too! Just like a pro, you can learn how to avoid unnecessary costs. You can avoid getting in and out of funds prematurely. You can make it a point of duty to diversify your investments. You can purchase indexes, and learn to keep an eye on exactly what is yours, and learn how to properly allocate assets. You can come to understand that making money in this business is not about picking stocks, but about proper allocation of assets. We'll get into how you can do this as we move along with this book.

If you want the very best, then you've got to keep in mind that you must keep expenses to a minimum. If you're to believe that a manager has consistently beat the market, do not just go by word of mouth, but ask to see actual, verified records. Choose an ETF company that you know is reputable. Always make sure you've got a couple of index funds invested along with your active funds.

The Downside of ETFs

It's not enough to cover the pros of ETFs. Let's take a look at the very real cons as well, so you can make a well-informed decision about whether you want your money to go into ETFs, and just how much of your money you want invested in this product.

The thing about ETFs is that the chances are you'll have to pay some fees in commissions, for each time you open and close, or short or go long on an ETF. The good thing though, is that the commissions have been dropping rapidly over the years. However, it would not do to ignore commissions just because of this drop. Not all commissions are low, and even the low ones can really stack up over time. So be on the lookout for that.

There's a fair chance that thanks to the fact that the markets are now open and available to you whenever you want, you might be prone to over trading. You might assume, like most people do, that there's nothing important about entries and exits, and that the longer and more often you remain in the markets, the more you are likely to grow your account. The only thing that will grow is that feeling of excitement within you, and if you're unfortunate, the hole in your account will increase exponentially as well, if you just walk into the market and start triggering buys and sells with no strategy in mind.

There are certain times when underlying securities in your ETF trade a bit below or above the price of the index they are supposed to mirror. This is not unusual, and you'll hear it referred to as "tracking error." There are also times when your ETF will be trading at a much lower or higher price than where it logically ought to be, when you consider all the securities that are in your ETF. When the price of your ETF is way above the actual value of your underlying securities, and you go short, you will hear this referred to as "selling at a premium." If the price of your ETF drops far beneath the actual value of your underlying securities when you go short, then you'll hear this called "selling at a discount." Tracking errors, selling at a discount, and selling at a premium all tend to happen a lot with bond funds, and funds based on foreign stocks. However, if you're dealing with the better funds available, you don't have to worry about this happening too frequently or to an outrageous point. If you're the kind of ETF investor who buys and holds, then you do not have to worry about any of this.

How Much Do You Need?

If you're going to make our portfolio out of ETFs, then you will need something around $50,000. If you have less than that, then it might be better for you to go with mutual funds, or better yet, do mutual funds with some ETFs as well. The one time you would go against this rule of thumb would be if you had a portfolio full of iShares ETFs, which are actually held at iShares, which implies you do not have to spend a dime on trading fees. In this case, it's okay to have a portfolio of just ETFs even if you have a small account to begin with.

One more thing I should add before I wrap up this chapter is that if you find you're constantly jumping into trades every single time the market says even the faintest "boo," then you would be much better off going with mutual funds, since with mutual funds, there isn't an imposition of fees for redeeming your funds within the short term. Also, you'd lose less money on account of being so impulsive.

CHAPTER THREE

Buying ETFs

In light of everything we have covered so far, you are probably thinking that you're in way over your head. Maybe it's time to put the book down. Clearly buying EFTs is for people who went to Harvard and Wharton. Well, you're wrong! It's really not as intimidating as you think it might be to buy ETFs. All you need are brokerage houses through which you can buy and sell any ETF you desire. So we're going to go over all of that, where to find them, the folks who are responsible for creating ETFs, the indexes which these ETFs are based off of, as well as the exchanges that make it possible for the trillions of ETF transactions which happen day in, day out.

Getting A Broker

You can't just walk into a store and buy ETFs like you would a lottery ticket or something. You've got to have an intermediary who will make the purchase on your behalf. That intermediary is known as a broker, or a brokerage house. You may also hear the broker being called a broker dealer. Not only will the broker buy ETFs for you, they'll also hold it. There are some really big brokers who will allow you purchase not just ETFs, but single stocks, bonds, mutual funds, and even options. You may be familiar with some of them already, like TD Ameritrade, Vanguard, and Schwab.

As I've already mentioned, you can trade ETFs the same way you trade stocks. You get charged similar commissions, and the rules are the same, for the most part. The trading hours are the same, based on Manhattan Island time, from 9:30 AM to 4:00 PM. Through your broker dealer, you can purchase a couple of shares, or a couple thousand share, or more. There's just one difference between stocks and ETFs: You can buy stocks straight from the company. This is rarely the case these days, but if you do, you might receive a certificate or some other form of documentation that proves you do indeed own stock from that company. With EFTs, you can't do that. You need a broker.

So, first things first, you've simply got to get a broker. You would be better off finding a broker who has diverse financial products, so that if you choose to invest in other stuff besides ETFs, it is super easy for you, especially when you need to keep track of monthly statements.

Questions That Need Answers

When you're opening an account, you've got to ask yourself whether you're creating a retirement account, or opting for a non-retirement account. Assuming you've chosen to opt for a retirement account, you've got to figure out the kind you need. Will it be a Roth IRA, regular IRA, or a SEP? If you're opening a non-retirement account, then things are a lot easier. You do not need to concern yourself with anything or regulation dealing with taxes. You also do not need to leave your money in there for a set period of time.

Next, you've got to figure out whether you would like a cash account, or a margin account. If you go with a margin account, that means that like a checking account, you've got overdraft protection. In other words, you have the ability to borrow from the account, or to buy securities like ETFs, even if you don't have a single dime to make the purchase right there and then. This is great, as long as you have self-control and aren't struggling with gambling. There are times when you might need to get a loan, and a margin account is great, and a lot cheaper when you weigh that option against a credit card. Another upside is the loan will more likely than not be tax deductible.

You'll also have to answer questions about who your beneficiaries are, titles, and whether you'd like to set up a joint account, which has rights of survivorship. Just make sure you name a beneficiary you won't regret. They're the one who'll get all your money when you pass on, no matter what your will says. You might will your ETFs to one person, but if the name that has been designated a beneficiary belongs to someone else, that's who it's going to. So, keep that in mind.

Other questions you will have to answer as you set up your account will be about your financial status, employment status, and risk appetite. Don't worry too much about these. It's standard practice for brokers to ask these things from their clients. For the most part, no one really pays attention to the personal stuff.

Making Your First Buy

As soon as your account has been set up and confirmed, you are just about ready to purchase your very first ETF! You have the option of making your purchase over the phone, or going online to do it yourself. You would be better off doing this on the internet, as it's the cheaper option. If you don't know how to go about placing your order, you can get the assistance of your broker, and they'll tell you what to do, step by step, without charging a cent.

Always keep the fees in mind. They might not look like much, but they can really add up over time and trades placed. Some brokers do not charge any commissions at all for placing trades, but don't let this fool you. One thing you will notice is that the second you get into a trade, you'll be in the red. That's because of a little thing called the **spread.** The spread is the difference between the bid price, and the ask price. The bid price is the price at which you buy, and it's usually different from the ask price, which is the price at which you sell. You always pay the spread, so you need to be mindful of that.

Little Fees, Big Dents

In order to prevent such little fees from making big dents in your account over time, here's a few things you need to do. First of all, trade well, not often. You'll hear this a lot in the trading world. What this means is that it's important for you to be strategic about your entries and exits as you trade. You don't just enter at market price, without thinking, unless the setup you want to see on your chart is exactly what's playing out Use limit orders and stop orders, so that you can better manage your risk. This way, you won't be making more trades than necessary.

You must also know how to work with your percentages. If you find that trading an ETF will cause you to cough up more than 0.5%, then don't bother with it. Say a trade will cost you $10, and you'd like to invest $1,500. If all you have is $1000 or below that, then it would be best if you buy yourself an index fund with no load. Better yet, I'd recommend that you wait until you're liquid enough to invest more. If you have the option of purchasing an ETF that comes with no commission, then that's better. Never mind that it might not seem as lucrative as the other one that has a commission attached. You can always invest in that later as your profits grow.

Be smart about your buying and selling. You want to make sure your trades are not eating into your profits, so please make sure you trade online only, and always buy the dip, and sell the rally. Keep in mind that if you are quite loaded, you can actually negotiate much better deals with your broker. They may not always say so, but if you've got about $10,000 and up, there might be a deal in it for you, such as getting your first 20 trades commission free. Just ask to see what they've got to offer.

Whatever you do, do not be rash about making your first trade. Don't assume just because you've read this book, you should liquidate everything you own, take the money and then dump them into a few ETF trades. You're going to get burned if you act rash. There are usually surcharges that are attached to liquidating your securities, so carefully consider which ones to offload that won't set you back by too much before you do so.

Placing Your Trade

Chances are if you've already traded some other financial instruments like stocks, or maybe even currencies, you won't have a problem figuring out how to trade ETFs. If you don't have any background knowledge, don't fret, I've got you. We'll go over the stuff you need to get familiar with, for now.

There are three basic orders you can place when trading. You've got the **stop order**, the **limit order,** and the **market order**. You can place a buy stop or a sell stop order. The buy stop order is placed above the current market price, and will not be triggered until the price of the ETF moves up and hits the level you've set the buy stop order for. When the price gets to your buy stop order, a buy trade is triggered and you're in the market. The sell stop order works the other way. Assume the market is going down. The sell stop order is placed below the current market price, and will not be triggered unless and until the price moves down toward the level you set the order at. Once it hits that level, a sell trade is triggered. You've also got **stop loss orders**, which basically is an instruction to your broker that once price has gone against your long (buy) or short (sell) position by a certain number of points, then the order must be closed in order to protect your money.

Next, you've got the limit orders. A buy limit order is placed below the current market price. It tells your broker to place a buy trade, as soon as the price of the ETF falls to that level. The sell limit is placed above the current market price, and instructs the broker to initiate a sell trade once the price rises and reaches your sell limit order, a sell trade is to be initiated.

The market order is pretty simple. It's basically an order to enter a trade at the current price the market is trading at. You can use this order with domestic ETFs that do not have crazy spreads and commissions, and preferably when the market is well underway and not acting erratically, like during news releases, or at market open (4:30 AM on weekdays, Manhattan Island time), or at market close (9:00 PM on weekdays, Manhattan Island time).

Best Time for Limit Orders

A limit order would serve you if the ETF you're buying or selling has a huge distance between the bid and the ask price, also known as the spread. This means you will not need to pay an exorbitant fee to get into a trade. You can also use limit orders when there is very little difference between the net asset value being held by your ETF, and the current market price of your ETF. This works pretty well for junk bond ETFs, or in stock ETFs, and all other kinds of ETFs that do not trade a lot of shares, particularly in choppy market conditions.

The only problem with limit orders that you need to keep in mind, though, is that sometimes, your trade will not be triggered, because the bid or the ask missed your order by a few points. If you want to make sure you do not miss out on the chance to get in on a trade using a limit order, then what you want to do is put your order in just a bit above or below where you would like to get in. Say you would like to place a sell limit order at $10.00, for 1000 shares. What you should do instead is place it at $9.99. It will cost you $10, but the good news is you still got in your trade, and if you called it right based on your strategy, you should be well on your way to making money.

What to Look for in A Broker

There are certain things you must be on the lookout for when you're choosing your broker. After all, they will be the ones responsible for carrying out your instructions when it comes to your money, so it only makes sense to do your due diligence when you're trying to figure out which broker should have the honor of holding on to your money.

First things first, they must have prices and fees that are reasonable. There's no point in using a broker that will drain your profits in fees and commissions. A good broker will also include deals that are irresistible and amazing — especially deals like getting to trade for free on particular ETFs. They should also give you top notch customer service You call them up anytime during business hours, and they must answer without having you wait, or wade through annoying voice prompts. They should also offer weekend and evening hours as well.

When you're choosing a broker, their website can tell you a story about whether or not they care about their clients. A broker's site should be intuitive, and easy to navigate.

You want a broker who will always give you solid advice. This is especially the case if you're new to trading EFTs or trading in general. Some brokers actually will assign someone to show you the ropes when it comes to trading.

You need a broker that has a service center as close to you as possible. This makes you feel like you're doing business with actual human beings, and not some cold, unfeeling machine.

One last thing to be on the lookout for is the financial capacity and strength of your broker. While all brokers are insured (the legit ones, anyway) the fact is that if a broker were to go under, you might find yourself in a bit of a pickle, as it may take a lot of time and resources to get your money back. Brokers are required by law to register themselves with the government. Upon registration, they are insured, thanks to the Securities Investor Protection Corporation, instantly. What this means for you as an investor, is that up to $500,000 of your investment is protected, in the event that the company goes under. A good broker will have supplemental insurance, to take care of the balance of your account not covered by SIPC. Do keep in mind that the SIPC is there to protect you if your broker goes poof, not if the markets were to suddenly drop against you.

Pricing

When choosing a broker, you would be wise to compare the prices before you finally settle on one. Some brokers will charge you anywhere from a couple bucks to $7 for each ETF trade, depending on how much money you've got to trade. However, if you're trading an ETF that is set up and managed by that particular broker you're with, you won't have to pay anything, most of the time. That said, do be careful! There are sometimes conditions that state that if you do not hold on to your trading positions for 30 days, you will be charged a whopping $30. Some other brokers might have you commit to trading only on certain days of the week.

A Broker Cocktail

I've already mentioned that it's great to choose a broker that offers all sorts of products, so you can take a look at all your investments at a glance. However, you have the option of mixing up your brokers. If you're going to do some mixing, then you'd better be really careful, so you're not left with a bitter taste in your mouth. It's great to mix brokers, provided you do it right. This will keep things flexible for you, and allow you access to the very best of EFTs for your portfolio.

One reason you might need a broker cocktail is that some brokers do not have certain mutual funds available for trading. However, they do have a ton of ETFs, and the more you can gain access to, the better for you.

When you mix your brokers, be sure you don't leave any gaps in your portfolio, and also make sure there is no overlap. You don't want to have an ETF with US stock funds only from more than one broker. It would be smarter for you to have an ETF provider who gives you US stock, another who gives you Japanese stock, and yet another who gives you European stock. Do note though that when you're combining a US growth fund, with a US value fund, or when you're mixing a US small cap fund with a US large cap fund to flesh out your portfolio, then it would be wise to choose ETFs from the same provider. The reason for this is that you'll find the definition of "growth," and "large," "small," and "value" varies from one provider to the next, and in this situation, mixing and matching may not be the best.

Getting to Know the Indexers

Right at the heart of each ETF, you will find an index. That's the very foundation of every ETF. There are some ETF providers who make use of the classic indexes, and others who create their own unique blends of underlying securities to create new ones. They do this along with the indexers who are seasoned.

Generally, if you want to know if any ETF is any good, then all you've got to do is take a look at the index it is connected to. It must be a solid one. That said, just because it's solid doesn't mean it's worth investing in, especially when you consider the associated costs, and whether or not said ETF is tax efficient. Here are the indexers responsible for the creation and recreation of the indexes that are mirrored by ETFs.

Dow Jones: Not only does this company publish *Barron's* and *The Wall Street Journal,* Dow Jones is also responsible for the development, maintenance, and licensing of over 3000 various market indexes, including the Dow Jones Industrial Average, which is a world-famous stock indicator.

Standard & Poor's: Standard & Poor's is owned by the publishing giant known as McGraw-Hill. The one thing it is well known for is rating credit. In addition to this, the company is responsible for the maintenance of several hundred indexes, along with the S&P 500, which you must have heard about at some point or the other on the news. There are over $1 trillion worth of assets that are sunk in S&P indexes. This is way more than the rest of the common indexes, put together. More than any other index, a lot of ETFs are based on the S&P 500, including Guggenheim equal weight ETFs, and an impressive number of Vanguard US ETFs, among others.

Russell: The Russell 1000 index is made up of the top 1000 US stocks. Yet, it is not quite as popular as the Dow Industrial and the S&P 500, especially when it comes to rating the performance of large cap. The Russell 2000 keeps track of the next top 2000 stocks in the United States market. Along with the Russell 1000, the Russell 2000 makes up the Russell 3000, which are the more popular indexes, though there are others, too.

MSCI: The MSCI is short for Morgan Stanley Capital International, as it used to be called. Now, it's not quite popular, but it has been making waves with ever increasing momentum as a choice indexer for ETF providers, providing indexes of all sorts, from bonds, and stocks, to hedge funds, and domestic and international securities.

Barclays: You may have heard of Lehman Brothers. For many years, it was the topmost indexer, when it came to fixed income investments. In 2008, Barclays Capital acquired Lehman Brothers just before the epic financial crisis that rocked the markets. Once that happened, the Lehman Brothers Aggregate Bond Index became known as the Barclays Capital Aggregate Bond Index.

CHAPTER FOUR

Your Portfolio

We're going to talk about the significance of large value and large growth stocks to your portfolio, among other things. Let's get into it.

Large Cap

When we talk about cap, which is short for capitalization, we're talking about the value of a company's stocks shares, combined. It can sometimes be a little tough to figure out where to draw the line between small cap, mid cap, and large cap. It's really very subjective. In general, you can think of small caps as companies that have capitalization anywhere from $250 million to $1 billion. For Mid-caps, the capitalization is anywhere from $1 billion to $5 billion. For the large cap companies, capitalization is above $5 billion. You have one more category called a micro-cap, and that is usually anything with capitalization from $50 million, to at the most, $250 million. Anything with capitalization beneath $50 million would be called a nano cap.

The Difference Between Growth and Value

There are so many different factors by which you could

figure out whether an ETF could pass as growth, or value. One factor reigns supreme, however, and that is called the P/E ratio, or the multiple. Essentially, this is the ratio of the price, to that of earnings.

To figure out the P/E ratio, you just have to divide the price of a stock by the earnings per share. If the Tudor Group has stock that's going for $50 a share, and they happened to earn $5 for each share of stock outstanding the previous year, then the Tudor Group's P/E ratio is 10.

What you need to keep in mind is that you can deem the company to be of **growth** if it has a high P/E, and you can think of it to be of **value** if it has a low P/E. Where investors have hopeful future projections for the former, which may or may not be based on reality, the latter is not considered as having much significance in business.

You'll find that each ETF has a P/E, which is basically a mirror of the collective P/E of the underlying securities, and this gives you a picture of whether or not your ETF is a growth EFT or of value. A growth ETF is usually full of companies that are doing so well they might as well take over everything in their industry and become a monopoly. A value ETF has got companies that are moseying along just okay, and have stock that has attractive prices that would be considered a steal.

When an investment professional is putting together her portfolio, she pays attention to the value or growth orientation of the stocks, as well as the cap size. The reason for this is simple. The likelihood of a portfolio doing well or poorly is based on where the portfolio happens to fall in terms of these two conditions. If you've got a mutual fund that has a lot of large growth stocks, for the most part, the mutual fund will rise and fall right along with that class of assets.

In fact, it's been found over time that at least 90 percent of an ETF's performance is tied to the asset class itself. This means that large cap growth funds will move in lock step with other similar growth funds that are large cap. If you've got a small cap value fund, it will do the same as others like it. This is the reason for the correlation of various funds.

Large Growth Stock Companies

These companies often enjoy the spotlight. You'll hear of them every day in the news. Everyone dreams of getting a job with companies like this. That said, just because everyone is talking about them, does not mean that they would be the best companies to invest in.

Compared to large value stocks, large growth stocks do not yield as much in returns as large value stocks do, annually. The rate for the former is 11.1 percent, while the latter is just 10.6 percent. In other words, you will get a lot more in dividends from large value stocks.

Since large value stocks have always proven to be more profitable than large growth stocks, and small caps have always done way better than large caps, what does this mean for you? Are large growth companies worth sinking your dollars into? Yes, they are. The thing about investment is that past performance is not indicative of future results. There is really no way to tell whether or not value stocks will keep doing better. The fact is that over the past decade, growth stocks have been catching up to value stocks, when it comes to small cap and large cap companies. There's no telling what the next decade will bring.

When it comes to your portfolio, I highly recommend that you make sure you've got a balanced mix of stocks from large value companies, and large growth companies as well. Let these make up at least 55% of your domestic stock. If you can take on more risk, you can easily drop the percentage a bit. No matter what you wind up allocating to the large cap stocks at home, it is best you put in about 40 to 50 percent of your investment in large growth companies. You can lean toward value a bit, but take it easy before you run the risk of ruin.

It's important that before you look for a large growth ETF to sink your funds into, you figure out whether or not you need one in your portfolio to begin with. Sure, you should get one, but you have to make sure that you've got a large enough portfolio that can easily be split up into various sectors and investments.

To Blend, or Not to Blend

This is the question. To be sure, the way to go is to invest in both large value stocks, and large growth stocks, ***but to do them separately***. The reason for this is simple. Annually, you get an opportunity to rebalance. As you do this, you can take out your profits safely, while eliminating your risk altogether. The thing to keep in mind is that the profit you make from the rebalancing had better be way beyond the costs you will have to pay for placing both trades (selling off shares from the profitable ETF, and then adding to the ETF that's not performing quite as well as the other.)

If you don't have a big enough portfolio to allow you still have profit after you're done rebalancing and paying off trading costs, then it might serve you better to go for a blend of growth, and value. If your portfolio is way too small to allow you to tweak your trades, then you would be better off blending everything, not just value and growth.

The Smoothie of Financial Investments

With a portfolio of $10,000 and below, you ought to consider mutual funds instead of ETFs. Alternatively, you should seek out a broker that will not charge you any fees for trading ETFs, if you can find one. The reason for this is that if you don't, you will find that the cost of trading will leave you broker than you've ever been. If you do know that you will not be trading over the next few years, then it's okay to go for an ETF portfolio, and to opt for the smoothie — meaning a blend of everything.

If you're going to go for everything, particularly in the class of domestic stocks, then you should consider the Vanguard Total Stock Market ETF (VTI), as well as the Schwab US Broad Market ETF (SCHB). These ones will give you really low trading costs, not above 0.054 percent.

Blending Small Cap and Large Cap

You might have less than $20,000, but more than $10,000. If you can simply do without it for a while, then think about simply compartmentalizing the domestic stock of your portfolio into small cap and large cap. You want a portfolio that is a diversified blend of large cap, and another portfolio that is a diversified blend of small cap. Consider the Vanguard Large Cap ETF (VV), as well as the Schwab U.S. Large Cap ETF (SCHX).

If your portfolio is over $20,000, then you can simply split it into two, with large cap value, and large cap growth options. Consider the Vanguard Growth ETF (VUG), and the Schwab U.S. Large Cap Growth ETF (SCHG) among other options.

Against the Grain

There are companies that do not have the notoriety in the media that others like Facebook and Alphabet Inc (Google) have. They may not be so posh, but the truth is that they do have some value to them. These companies are typically in industries that are considered slow growers, such as pharmaceuticals, insurance, and transport, among others. So, you can talk about companies like GlaxoSmithKline, Wal-Mart, Exon, and others. You've got to have these in your portfolio.

The reason you want these kinds of stocks in your portfolio, is that they happen to yield the very best returns consistently. In fact, you might want to consider making large value companies the lion's share of your portfolio.

There are those who believe that while it might not be apparent, there is some risk in going down the value investing road. The reasoning is that there's every chance for value stocks to sink way low, during times of economic crises. This is not enough of a reason to not get involved in value investing, if you ask me. Granted, during the financial crisis of 2008, the value stocks took a much harder hit to the nose than the growth stocks. However, this was the opposite of what went down in the meltdown that happened between 2000 and 2002. So, who's to say what will happen during the next market meltdown?

There are also those who believe that the reason value stocks of much better than growth stocks is that there are higher dividends paid out by the value companies, while growth companies are more likely to put their profit right back into the business, with the aim of making acquisitions, and developing new products. The thing to keep in mind about value stocks is that for the most part, at least in the past, value stocks are mostly just ignored. For this reason, they are quite cheap. Whenever anyone does remember value stocks, it's hardly ever with a fond sentiment. There's no surprise there, because it's been established that investors will always be a little over the top in their reaction to bad news, which means that the prices of value stocks are usually available for a steal, since the demand for them is quite low. Since the prices are low, smart investors come in and buy them at a discount, with the understanding that in spite of the lack of profits at the moment, it is very possible for these companies to turn into gold eventually. However, you would be better off investing in large value stocks by buying the index, and not the actual shares. Unless you've got Warren Buffet on speed dial, or you both use the same financial oracle or something — in which case, you would need to read this book.

As you look into ETFs more, you'll find that there are

quite a few that are worthy of your attention. Check out the Vanguard Value ETF (VTV), iShares Russell 1000 Value ETF (IWD), Vanguard Mega Cap 300 Value Index ETF (MGV), the Schwab U.S. Large Cap Value ETF (SCHV), and the iShares Morningstar Large Value ETF (JKF), among others. Make sure that as you allocate your resources to large cap stocks, which are domestic, you put in about 50 to 60 percent towards large value. No more, no less than that range will do.

Small Value and Small Growth

You should definitely consider adding small value and small growth company stocks to your portfolio as well. Just imagine if you'd been quick on the draw and invested before Microsoft, or Facebook, or Uber got where they are today. You'd be a very, very happy camper, with a lot of cash in your account. This is a very good reason for you to invest in small value and small growth companies. The stock of these companies happen to have a total market value from between $300 million to as high as $1 billion. You'll find that they tend to be in the tech space, and have some patent or product that is very hot, and possibly revolutionary. Some of these companies will win in the end, becoming big ones, which make you big ones as well, if you invest.

That said though, there are way more losers than there are winners out there. It would be absolutely nuts for you to pick a single small value or small growth company and ink all your funds into it, because you run the risk of losing it all. Now, if you had more than enough money to burn, you might want to consider putting your money in a number of them, and this would exponentially increase your odds of making money, based on historical events.

Over the past hundred years, small cap stocks have continued to do way better than large cap stocks. They also tend to have a lot more volatility as well. When it comes to the amount of profits you receive for each unit of risk you take on, you'll find that small caps are the better options every time. That said though, it's not every small cap you want to put money into.

You should turn your sights to small cap value stocks, and not small cap growth socks. It's a bit of a mystery why these do better than the small growth stocks, but the stats over time have shown that your money will work better for you if you invest in small cap value stocks. While small cap growth stocks have brought in 11.5 percent a year for the past couple of decades, small cap value stocks have brought in a whopping 15 percent a year. This does not mean you should completely shun small cap growth stocks. You should make your portfolio diverse, by adding them in. There have been times when the small cap growth stocks have done better than the small cap value stocks. We must not completely count out the possibility of small cap growth stocks doing well as well.

Portioning Your Portfolio for Small Cap

If you happen to have a portfolio that is below $20,000, then you should definitely look into investing in a blend of small cap value stocks and small cap growth stocks. Make sure your portfolio does not have more than 20 percent of the small cap domestic stocks. It's important you do not go over this number, or else the trading costs will eat you alive. You can go a little higher once your portfolio has shown enough growth to allow you to do that.

Some small cap blends of ETFs to look at would be the Vanguard Small Cap (VB), the Schwab U.S. Small Cap (SCHA), and the iShares S&P Small Cap 600 (IJR). Just for the record, some small value stocks are those like Arthur J. Gallagher & Co., Snap-On Inc, and Alaska Air. Small cap growth stocks would include companies like ISIS Pharmaceuticals, Zebra Technologies, Toro Co, and Maximus Inc. You may find that there are certain companies about to go belly up, and others dealing with lawsuits and other challenges. There's a lot of risk, to be sure! But the potential for rich rewards is worth it.

In the end, it is best for you to make sure that you've got a nice blend going on in your portfolio all the time. That way, even if things are going to hell in one sector, you can rest assured that things are working out perfectly well in another, and this will keep your account at break-even at least, if not consistently growing, until things settle down.

CHAPTER FIVE

LET'S TALK TRENDS AND TOOLS

The trend is your friend. Until it ends. Then you turn around and make it your friend again. If you're going to invest wisely, then you've got to make it your duty to be able to recognize trends. There's no way around that. You've got to know when you're in a bull market — an uptrend — and when you're in a bear market — a down trend. Also, you've got to be able to identify when there's no trend, meaning the market has been moving sideways, or consolidating within a specific range of prices, bouncing up and down in that range, and going nowhere.

If you're hearing about the trend of the market being bullish or bearish from your friend's wife at some fancy dinner, then chances are all the profits to be made from that trend have already been booked, and anyone who tries to get in at that point will be burned, because they will either be buying the top of a new down trend, or selling the bottom of a new uptrend. In other words, they will be moving against the market, and bleeding dollars every step of the way. This is why you need to learn to figure out when a trend is starting, when it's ending, when it's only pausing, and when it has done a 180.

For this reason, the buy and hold strategy is just plain silly. Markets don't go up forever. They don't go down forever either. Imagine you had been buying everything, and then suddenly the market starts a downtrend and maintains that downtrend for 7 solid years. What would you do, then? And what if you don't have enough capital to weather those years? What happens then? You could have made money going short, but because someone's accountant said to "buy and HODL," you lost big time. This is why I advocate being a trader, and not an investor.

Trading Versus Investing

Sure, the title of this book says "investing," but the truth is I see trading as investing **smarter** than simply investing. Where an investor will just buy and hold hoping that things will continue to be on the up and up, the trader is quick to follow the trend as he sees it. The trader trades based on what she sees, not what she thinks is going to happen. If you're looking at your screen and you see the trend has been moving from the top left corner to the bottom right corner, then that is clearly a bear market. So why would you want to buy that, unless you know that the price is approaching an old, low point from which it turned around and continued up? It makes no sense.

All you need to do to make money in any market condition is to be long when the trend is up, be short when the trend is down, and be out when the trend is choppy. It's simple, so don't feel intimidated.

An Argument Against "Buy and Hold"

You may think that the buy and hold strategy is something that is tested and trusted. It may have worked in the past, but I promise you, that's not where it's at right now. It's a dead thing. Let go, before it drags you and your account balance down. To give you some understanding of how terrible this is, in 2008, Buffet himself allegedly lost a whopping $16 billion — and he's a buy-and-holder. Sure, not everyone has $16 billion to lose, but the point is this is a terrible strategy that can only work for you if you have deep, deep pockets to help you withstand the drawdown you will inevitably experience, before the markets turn around and go back up again. Besides the money you lose, you also lose time. Time that could have been spent making more money by selling, not buying.

About Sideways or Choppy Markets

You should avoid trading when the market is moving sideways, unless you feel like losing some money because you're some sort of masochist or something. Sideways markets can be exhausting, and can wear down not just your account, but your mind and emotions as well. It's like plodding through snow, or sand, or sandy snow that is also sinking sand. You're just not going to make much progress, if any, it will be downhill. If you buy and hold and you hit choppy markets, who is to say the markets won't just chop on for a very long time, when you could have been making money in markets that are actually moving, even if they're going **down** and not up, like you've been advised is best? Imagine buying, and then you hold through the chop, watching your money, and then you're hit with a down trend, but since you're team bullish for life, you hold on and watch your money dwindle away for years. Then it's finally back up, but you're not so sure price won't just chop again. It just makes no sense to be forever long. Adapt with the markets. Time is way too short, and the emotional drain is just not worth it.

Emotions

You must master your emotions, before you make money in ETF investing. The only way for you to trade without having to deal with mastering your emotions, is to automate your trading strategy. This book is not about that, but you can look that up.

When it comes to investing, you must be aware of two emotions: Fear, and Greed. Fear keeps you from getting into a position because you have been burned way too many times, probably as a result of having a terrible strategy, or not following your rules. Greed is what keeps you in the trade when you should be out, or makes you take on positions that are simply way too much for the size of your portfolio.

One thing you must learn to do is make friends with losses. Be okay with them. This also means you should learn to accept them quickly and early. You must be okay with getting out of your trade at a moment's notice, once you realize you went in at the wrong time, or you're in the wrong position.

It matters as well that you know exactly why you got into each position, all the time. You need to know what it is you saw and thought that made you enter a buy position or a sell position, and before you pull the trigger, you must know exactly what it is you will take as a sign that you need to get out, whether you're in profits or not.

It's not going to be easy, I'll tell you that. We're human anyway, and we are very emotional creatures. Even the most logical of us are dominated by the fear of making decisions which would be deemed emotional, and studies have shown no matter how reasonable our rationale is for doing what we do, it all comes down to emotion as the key motivator. So, to deal with this, I will offer you a strategy that will help you, regardless of your emotions. This strategy will involve making use of the 200-period exponential moving average.

You must have a wide range of various sectors you can invest in. This way, you won't need to just hope that one market continues to trend one way or the other forever, or that it never experiences a bout of chop. You know yo can always take a peek at other markets, and see how they are doing, and then join the trend early. Following the trend is how you protect and grow your capital, in both bear and bull markets.

Risk

There is nothing without risk, and the market is no exception. It is not risk that is the problem, but simply the emotions which run us, leading us to make disastrous decisions. Rather than sell, you may have felt fear that kept you from clicking the button. Rather than close, you may have felt hope that the price would turn around and go your way, and your hope became the undoing of you and your account balance. Rather than stop trading, you're riding on the high of winning trade after trade, so you go in for another one, and use a bigger position size than you should have. It's okay. This is not unusual, especially when you're just starting out with trading and investing. However, it's important to do something about our emotions, to curb our fears and enthusiasm, if we hope to win at this game.

The real risk you must avoid here is trading without a clearly defined strategy in mind. You cannot just buy and sell because your gut says so, or because Mercury is in retrograde and your personal psychic says this is a good time for you to make millions you've always dreamed of. Just as risky is having a strategy, yet never sticking to your plan when it's time to execute.

The fact is that the markets will always be risky. The only thing you can do is to mitigate your risks, keeping them as low as you can. You cannot tame or control the market. You do not own the funds to do that. However, you can at least control the way you respond to it at any given time.

Greed, Fear, Money

Remember the 90s, when everyone went nuts about any stock that was tied to the internet? I bet you do. Everyone was acting out of greed as they bought, not pausing to think about the fact that that news about tech and internet being the future was not just random reporting, but reporting with an agenda: Drive up the value of the stocks. A lot of people who fell for it and didn't get out when they should have wished they had done their due diligence. Some of them refused to set a stop loss order, believing that things would turn around. Instead, they watched their portfolios dwindle into oblivion when the crash happened. Till date, there are still those who fancy themselves some sort of trading Indiana Jones, and never set a stop loss or use the correct position sizing.

There's also the fact that getting into this and never being burned can lead to a false sense of security and bravado, a false assumption that every trade will be a win. This feeling makes you take silly risks that will come back to bite you in the derriere, eventually.

Fear is just as bad too. So, you lost a trade here and there, and then you see a great setup, but now you don't want to jump in. Why? You're worried this one will be another loser. You come back days later and see that the price has gone where you thought it would. If only you had gotten in! You lament. If you size your positions the right way, and set a stop loss where it should be, then you should be able to trade with no loss of sleep.

Keep in mind that most people tend to never think about risk, unless and until they actually lose money. Most people also lose money. The moral of the story? Try not to be like most people. Figure out your risk early, and don't jump into just any setup unless it has all the criteria you want to see.

Risk Tolerance

You must know what your risk tolerance is. Some people can handle a lot, while others are risk averse. If you want more rewards, then you need to be willing to take on more risk. If you want to make 20 percent, then you had better be sure you can also handle a loss as much as that as well. If you keep your risk conservative, say at 5 percent, then you'll last longer in the game.

Risk tolerance is simply how comfortable you are with losing a part of your capital, or even all of it. The more risk the more you are open to disaster. Once you know what your risk tolerance is, you can then move ahead. No one can tell you what that should be. It's completely up to you to figure it out. Thankfully, most ETF providers will offer you calculators online, so that you can know right off the bat how much you're comfortable losing. This is where the importance of understanding the trend comes to play, because you can then get a better handle of your total risk, and work on creating a safety net.

With the 200-period exponential moving average, you will know immediately which side of the market you need to be on. It will be the line in the sand that tells you to get out of a trade, when things move from one side of the average, to the other side. With this strategy, we are not interested in picking tops or bottoms. We're not trying to predict. We're not trading based on gut, or thought. We're trading what we see, and nothing more.

There are two kinds of risks, other than the market risk, that is. You've got **inflation risk,** and **liquidity risk.** Inflation risk is the chance that your assets values will drop over time, as inflation causes the purchasing power of a certain currency to dip, while liquidity risk is the chance that you will not be able to sell the securities you've got, on account of a lack of market liquidity. You run into liquidity risk when you're trading markets with low volume, or you're working with markets that are only just emerging.

Just keep in mind that your ability to make the moolah is largely dependent on how well you can deal with risk, fear, and greed as well. There's a chance you'll be swayed by the news on the TV or in the papers. There's a chance we will come to choose gut over everything else that is pointing to some other direction. However, you must learn to discipline yourself. The market does not care about your gut feelings. Maybe you do create your own reality, but leave that psychology at the door when it comes to trading, because the market is the market, and it respects no one. You must be level headed. You cannot trade when you're mad, or upset, or intoxicated. You must not get married to your positions. Be a flake. Be willing to dump them at a moment's notice, without even as much as a glance back.

How Much Time?

Knowing your risk tolerance is not enough. You need to also know how much time you've got to wait till you reap the profits. After all, the whole point of this is to make money you can enjoy, is it not? So, it's important you know just how long it will take you before you achieve your investment goals. If you've got more time on your hands, then you've got enough time to weather the bad times in the market. If you're a little too close to retirement, you're not going to leave your money in the stock market. If you're saving up for something you plan to get years later, you're not about to gamble with your money by taking huge risks. So, figure out where you are in life, and what you want out of it, then make sure that the portfolio you sculpt factors in your current state of affairs, in addition to your risk appetite.

Finding the Trends

It's not easy to get it right one hundred percent of the time with every trade. You cannot always buy low and sell high, in reality. So, what is the next best thing you can do? It's simple. Figure out the trend, and then get in. If you notice the trend has change before you get your profits, you get out. Straight to the point. The way we're going to monitor trends is with the 200-period exponential moving average. I like to keep my charts simple and clean, and his has worked for me for decades, with no problems at all.

You may or may not be familiar with what a moving average is, but I promise you'll understand when we're through with this chapter. So, let's talk about what a moving average is. This is a tool used by technical traders, to determine the current trend of price. The moving average plots a line along your chart. This line is based off of the closing prices of the past X number of periods — the X being variable. In our case, we're going to set that number of periods to 200. What this means is that the line you're looking at on your chart represents the average of closing prices over the past 200 days, or 200 4-hour candles, or 1 hour or 30-minute chunks of time, depending on what time frame you choose to trade with. You can ask your broker for help in setting up your charting program, so that it plots a 200-period exponential moving average on your charts.

What the moving average does is that it shows you what the markets are doing in the moment. It lets you know if they're moving up, or down, or if they're ranging. Now, this is not necessarily foolproof. Sometimes you will get false signals. The key is figuring out how to filter them, and above all else, managing your risk so that the false signals do not even scratch your account.

In an uptrend, one thing you will notice is that the market makes higher highs, and higher lows, as it moves on up. What this means is that price will make a strong push up, a little move down knows as a "retracement," and then another strong push up, past the previous high where price paused before. Then it will make another retracement, and on and on. In a down trend, price makes a strong push down, a small retracement back up, and then another push down, and then another retracement, breaking new lows, on and on, ad nauseum, ad infinitum. Until the trend is over, of course.

One of the telltale signs that a trend is over is when a swing has been broken. What is a swing? It's simply the points on the chart where the price of an asset retraced to, before continuing on its way up, or down. So, if price has been making lower and lower swings, and then suddenly price moves up enough to break past the most recent swing low, then there might be an end to the down trend and the start of a new uptrend — or some choppiness, at worst.

When is the market moving sideways, or ranging, or consolidating, or choppy? It's when you notice that price has been moving in between a fixed range of prices, and that no new swing lows or swing highs are being made.

Rules of The Trend Following Strategy

Here are the rules:

1. Use the daily time frame, and nothing less.

2. When price goes over the 200 exponential moving average, open a buy position.

3. When the price goes under the 200 exponential moving average, open a sell position.

4. When you feel overwhelmed with emotions, close your trades, shut off your computer, come back tomorrow.

Now, as you look at various charts, you will notice it's not every trade that will win, following these rules. You'll notice that you will win some, and you'll lose some, not because you were wrong, but because the trend was only for the short or midterm, and you were in there too long. However, this is way better than some random financial news reporter telling you that it's time to go long, or that the markets have turned bearish, and then you acting on that very late tip.

Kinds of Moving Averages

You have the Simple Moving Average (SMA), which sums up the prices of the past 200 trading days, and then divides that sum by 200. You've got the Exponential Moving Average (EMA), which places more emphasis on the more recent prices. This means it reacts a lot faster than the SMA. There are other moving averages as well, such as the smoothed moving average, and the linear weighted moving average, but for the purpose of this book, we'll keep things simple and focus on the exponential moving average, as it gives faster signals. The only downside to faster signals is that sometimes you can enter or exit a little too soon, and have to deal with a whipsaw, but since we're working with the daily time frame and nothing less, you do not need to be overly bothered with whipsaws.

Graceful Exits

Most investors, even the very best ones, still struggle with exits. Remember greed? It comes into play, as they wonder whether or not they should hold on a little bit longer, see just how much more juice they can get out of the trend. Others struggle with figuring out when a losing trade is a losing trade. It doesn't help when you also pay attention to fundamentals — meaning news about the instruments you're trading — and those fundamentals are saying you should stay in. it's for this reason that I am a strictly technical trader. I only pay attention to the news to make sure I'm not getting into a trade during overly volatile times as economic events and news releases.

For a graceful exit, what I do is simple. If I'm in a buy, once the price moves beneath the 200 exponential moving average, I exit my buy, and go short. If I'm in a sell, and the price goes above the 200 exponential moving average, I exit my sell, and go long. I don't care what the fundamentals are saying. I don't pay attention to anything besides what I can see, and that is exactly what I trade. You can learn to do this too. Yes, there will be choppy times, and they can be annoying, but it doesn't do to dwell on the past. Just move on to the next trade.

Think of your cash as being an asset class of its own. Once you find yourself in a whipsaw, you can consider moving on to another ETF. You don't have to keep buying and selling the same one thing, waiting for it to finally pick a side and move. You must always use a stop loss order, as this will protect you from any sudden moves against your position. Also, learn to take your profits. You can't go broke taking profits!

Bursting Bubbles

The market has always and will always create bubbles. The one way to protect yourself is to make sure you have a clearly defined strategy for exiting your trades. Always get out the second you notice that the price has gone the opposite way on your 200-period exponential moving average. You can have your broker assist you with setting up notifications that go straight to your phone, so you know when it is time to get out of, or into a trade.

It's easy to give in to the anxiety and excitement caused by the volatile movements of the markets, but you've got to keep that in check. You could get out of the markets and just wait out the choppiness for a bit, but once that's over and there's a trend again, you need a plan to get back in the business of making money.

The fact is the market is always doing one of the things, so be on the lookout for the chance to sell, and to buy. If you allow fear to get in the way, you will miss out. I'm not asking you to give in to the fear of missing out or FOMO and jump into trades willy nilly either. I'm simply asking you to be ready to pull the trigger.

Historically speaking, bear markets are followed by bull markets, and vice versa. When the market is going down in one sector, you will invariably see some other sector that is booming. So, if you're not open to selling, you can always be on the lookout for buying opportunities. All you need to do is be willing to give your trades the time to develop, and don't exit unless and until you see the signal to do just that.

Following the trend will net you consistent profits and a fatter portfolio in the long run, as long as you stick to it. It's much better than just shooting in the dark and hoping you hit something this time.

Investment Tools

If you're going to make a killing investing in ETFs, then you must be willing to set yourself up with the required tools to help you do just that.

Get the News

There are two three kinds of traders, or investors, if you'd prefer. There are the fundamental traders, who make use of news reports or "fundamentals," or "funny mentals," as they are pejoratively called, to make their trading decisions. Then there are the technical traders, who trade based on technical indicators and price action clearly visible on the chart. Finally, there are those who trade a mix of both strategies, to varying degrees. I've already said what I use the news for, and beyond that, I couldn't care less what it has to say. That doesn't mean you can't use it! There are traders and investors who are purely fundamentalists, and the do very well.

It's not a bad idea to be aware of what's happening in the market. I don't mean you've got to stay glued to the tube, but you can make use of some awesome sites on the internet, like Market Watch, Smart Money, and Yahoo! Finance, which I've mentioned before.

With these websites, you'll know what is going on in each country, and in each sector. They are often updated as things happen over the course of the day, so you don't miss a beat. You can also check out sites like Investing.com. They have a wonderful app that allows you to keep track of economic events all over the world, and can even notify you when price hits certain levels on the instruments you're watching.

For websites which deal specifically with ETFs, you can check out Seeking Alpha, Green Faucet, ETF Trends, and Morningstar. With these websites, you'll know all there is to know about ETFs, as well as innovations in the industry, and the effect of economic and financial events on ETFs.

Technical Analysis

This is useful, because this is the way you figure out how well or how poorly ETFs are doing, in the short, medium, and long term. You can take a look at relative strength, and relative weakness. You can learn about expense ratios, holdings, trend lines, and so much more. There are websites that cater to this. The ETF Trends website has an ETF trends Analyzer, which will allow you to chart your ETFs and see what the 200 day and 50 day moving averages are doing. You also get a table that shows you in depth analysis on ETFs, which have no less than $50 million in terms of assets. You can also see what the performance of ETFs have been for the day, and over the long haul, as well as the annual high, and trendlines.

ETF Connect is another website that allows you to view ETFs sorted according to size, current distribution rate, discount, and premium. You can also view the ETFs sorted out according to sponsor and class. The site also offers you charting, and the ability to track portfolios.

ETF Screen will give you a snapshot of the day to day movements of ETFs. This movement is updated at 15-minute intervals, and shows the way they have performed over the past year, six months, three months, month, and five days as well.

ETF Providers of Note

If you would like to learn even more about ETFs, then look no further than your ETF provider, and they can teach you about trading volume, assets, the top holdings, and even expense ratios. You can get all of this info on their website, if it's a good ETF provider. Here are some you should definitely check out:

- **iShares**, which offers podcasts and presentations on demand.
- **PowerShares,** which has an impressive number of guides you will find useful. They also have some really great webcasts to teach you more about ETFs.
- **Morningstar**, which has a list of 25 of the top performing holdings, as well as their weighting. You can also get info on their performance, yield, expense

ratio, assets, and lots more.

- **State Street Global Advisors**, which has got SPDR University so you can learn more. They also have incredible resources with commentary on the market, presentations, webcasts, articles, and even research papers.

Charting

You need to have a charting tool, if you're going to be able to see the trends, and notice patterns that play out on your ETFs. For this, here are some tools I recommend:

- **Yahoo! Finance**. This will allow you to take a look at both the simple moving average and exponential moving average, including the performance of ETFs from as recent as 5 days ago to as far back as 10 year ago till date. You can even look at the funds' performances right from their inception. Ou also have the option of creating a portfolio for free, putting in points to sell, and keeping an eye on trendlines.
- **ETF Trends** will allow you view the charts for any ETF you want, and will allow you to customize the view a needed. You can also look at the 200 moving average on whatever time frame you want.
- **Stock Charts** will let you look at some charts for free. If you want more, you can pay to subscribe. With a paid subscription, you can even send the chart to your PC as an image file, among other things.
- **Big Charts** will give you the most detailed charts for every major fund and index.

You will find that the bulk of these tools are completely free of charge, while some offer premium stuff you can pay for. Just shop around and see what will do nicely for you.

CHAPTER SIX

International Investment

A round the globe, there are nations that have had to deal with challenges, and successes, economically speaking. These country's economies have a ripple effect that affects not just their domestic economies, but the entire global market as well. It's not hard to see that rises and falls in the market are cyclical, and affect one and all.

If you think you would be better off not adding funds from these countries to your portfolio, then you would be doing yourself a great disservice. America may be a superpower, but the fact is that the rest of the world actually accounts for almost 70 percent of the world's market cap. Yes, the US has the lion's share of this market, but there are developed and developing nations who are also at the table.

Companies are affected by economic issues, currency, and trade, in so many ways. As time goes by, nations all over the world will have opportunities as well as challenges which will affect their markets in good ways and bad ways as well. It is a very uncommon scenario to have every single economy and country of the world doing incredibly well at the same time, or to have them all going through some struggles at the same time. It just doesn't happen. What that means for you is that you have a golden opportunity to diversify your portfolio and make money outside of domestic funds, by figuring out which countries are doing well and trending the way you want them to go.

Some countries are doing great, while others are doing poorly. That's just the way the cookie crumbles. Consider the fact that today, more than ever, there has been an intermingling of ever nation's economy, in such a way that we have all come to depend on one another for one thing or the other. There is opportunity everywhere, whether it's a developed nation, or one that is still finding its feet.

Back in 2008, the year of the financial crisis, this was the order in which the global market cap was owned, starting from the highest to the lowest: The United States of America had 29.9 percent (a huge drop from 43.7 percent which was the rate as at 2004); Japan had 8.2 percent; the United Kingdom had 6.8 percent; China had 5.4 percent, while the rest of the world accounted for the global market cap. What these numbers have been telling us is that the rest of the world is catching up to the United States. We're probably not going to remain at the top for much longer, truth be told.

This all begs the question, should you sink your investments into a market that is already developed, or an emerging market like China's for example? This is not unlike trying to figure out whether small cap or large cap is the way to go, or whether you should choose value over growth. When you think about it, the developed markets have peaked. The chances of them doing any better than they already are pretty slim, in my honest opinion. On the other hand, the markets which are yet emerging, blazing new trails, are, as Drake would say, starting from the bottom. This means they have a lot of room to grow, and if you get in on the action, you could reap incredible rewards when they do become successful ad developed.

A Chance to Grow in Emerging Markets

The global markets right now are looking really sexy, and for good reason. They offer you, the investor a very unique opportunity to grow, especially where domestic markets have not been able to. Add in the fact that money and tech are starting to really move around the globe, and you can see how economies that were once isolated have been roped into a cohesive, global one. If you would like to get in on the action, you can think about compartmentalizing the markets as regional, and country-based markets.

Emerging markets are as exhilarating as they are bothersome, to be honest. Their growth is rapid, and they still have so much more room to expand and become even more. This is what makes them so attractive to investors, apart from the fact that when things are not working out so well at home, the tendency is to look outside for greener grass. I am of the opinion that we should do a lot more than simply look to them when things aren't working out well at home, as they have so much, they can offer!

Emerging Markets and Frontier Markets

An emerging market is one which is currently undergoing

reforms, as well as developments. For this reason, while China is making amazing leaps and bounds in terms of its economy, it is still classed as an emerging market on account of the fact that it is yet developing its policies and reforms. This is also why you won't hear of a superpower like Britain being called an emerging market, since it is not likely to make a lot of changes to its current policies, especially in terms of its economy.

Brazil, Russia, India, and China, or the BRICs as they are known, are a group of super economies with emerging markets. According to a 2003 report by Goldman Sachs, these economies will be a lot wealthier than a lot of major economies, come 2050.

You've also got frontier markets, which are even smaller than emerging markets. These ones happen to be the furthest away from the center of the world's economy. We're talking about nations like Zimbabwe, Vietnam, and Thailand. These are usually having to contend with political strife, ridiculous inflation, and weakened currencies. Their economies are swayed by every whim. There is the chance for very juicy profits, but as I've already mentioned before, there's attendant risk with that too.

2002 to 2007 saw an annual gain of 25 percent in the diversified stock funds of the emerging markets. When you put that side by side with the 5 percent pulled in by the Dow Jones Industrial Average, it's not hard to see your money would be better served if you include emerging markets in your portfolio.

Riding the Dragon

Investors have learned the hard way that when you count out a frontier market, or an economy like China's, you miss out a whole lot on the growth that would have no doubt made a nice impact on your portfolio. With the modern technology we have, it has become even easier to get involved in emerging markets, and there is no better way to get in on the action than through ETF.

Once you have a solid trend following strategy like the one, I have proffered in this book, you can and will cash in on the action. Imagine you already knew all of this, and you were right in place to take advantage of the Chinese bullish dragon run that began in the 2000s.

Just like it was with the era of tech investments, where people thought you could just choose some random stock and get millions instantly, a lot of people thought they could just choose whatever international stock bond out of a pile in a hat, run with that, and make trillions. What they did not factor in their decisions, however, is that there is an awful lot of volatility in emerging market funds — particularly anything to do with the Yen, or the Dragon, as it is fondly called. What would then happen was investors would buy at the worst possible moments, and sell when they shouldn't.

The rise of China is an amazing one. As soon as diplomatic relations were normalized between China and America by President Carter, there was a freer flow of exports, and this proved to be a wonderful thing for the land of the free and the home of the brave. All it took was a little over 25 years, and China had gone from poor and impoverished to a market that thrives globally. At the highest point, China had a gross domestic product of 11 percent per annum. It spent dollars in the trillions, in order to reform its infrastructure, and modernize everything. Then, just before the Olympics, China got a little too carried away with shopping.

By October 20007, China's stock market had peaked, after growing up to 400% more over a five-year period. Those who had bought stock in companies that traded with the Yen were smiling to the bank so hard it could blind you. The downside though, is those who were in the markets who believed buy and hold was the only way to go, got ripped to shreds. 2008 rolled around, and China took a massive hit in its economy and market. It had to deal with a reduced interest in real estate, fuel scarcity, and other disruptions in the state of their affairs. On account of this, the iShares FTSE/Xinhua China 25 Index FXI (China's largest ETF) dropped down by a staggering 65.8 percent, with October 20007 being when it saw its all-time high. If you had been following the trend following strategy I've given, you would have reaped your profits, and exited early when the price dipped beneath the 200-day exponential moving average in January 2008.

What to Know About Investing in Emerging Economies

At this point, it should be pretty obvious to you why a trend following strategy is the best way to go. The truth of the matter is whether it's commodities, forex, etfs, mutual funds, indexes, or whatever, there is no market that just keeps going up, or just keeps going down. The emerging economy is no exception to this rule, which is why it makes sense to simply follow the trend, and take the opportunities as you see them, using the 200 exponential moving average.

Keep in mind that emerging markets are incredibly volatile. What this means for you is that you have the chance to make money in both up and down markets. You just need to have a solid entry and exit strategy, so that you can be in and out of the markets, and keep reaping the profits.

BRIC Money

From 2003 to 2007, Brazil, Russia, India, and China performed astoundingly well. Any funds that were invested in these countries gave the investors at least 70 percent in returns, if not more. However, this was short lived. By the time 2008 came around, there was a global crisis involving credit that affected most of the world.

It was once thought that the BRICs economies were going to get so strong that they would eventually split off on their own, but that has not been the case. All economies are one way, or another tied to one another, as all countries rely on one another for various things. On account of the surge in oil prices, the decrease in lending, and the reduction of disposable income available, a lot of these companies got hit pretty badly in 2008.

In spite of that, though, there's still a chance for you to get on board, as prices have dropped low enough for you to buy them at a steal, using the right strategy. The smart play is to look for signs of strength, and get in on the trade once you get the signal from the 200-day exponential moving average to do so. This is not uncommon knowledge, and that's why the whole world is looking at India and China, especially with a lot of interest, as these two could very well become a challenge to the American economy over time.

Global ETFs

Global ETFs, or international ETFs, happen to be a real crowd favorite in the ETF world. You have several choices, and it all comes down to how much exposure you're comfortable with. You could choose to focus on ETFs from certain regions, or those from particular countries within a set region — like BRICS. You could also choose a particular country, if you like.

You could choose to focus on a particular market that is emerging, using a single-country fund. This will give you lots of volatility, and lots of reward, should the country you choose wind up doing well.

Your other option is to choose a particular region, or a group of emerging markets by making use of a broad-based fund. What this does is it keeps your risk spread out over several emerging markets, while allowing you to enjoy the volatility from each one.

International, Developed Markets

You can look at ETFs from other developed countries as well, if you would like something to keep your portfolio nice and stable. The thing about already developed countries is that they are pretty much all set, and are not interested in growing any further, since they are all grown already. So, you can be certain things will stay stable. Also, they do have much less risk than emerging or frontier market funds, since they are less likely to experience a terrible decline overnight.

Just like with emerging markets, you can choose funds based on regions, single-country funds, and even funds that are all-encompassing. If you want the broader funds, then consider the Claymore/Zacks Country Rotation (CRO). This one has 200 stocks, from companies on the international scene, which developed international exchanges have listed, and with Singapore, Australia, Sweden, and Spain as the exposure countries. You could also check out the BLDRS Developed Markets 100 ADR (ADRD), with weightings in Japan, the United Kingdom, Switzerland, and France.

If you are more interested in the regional developed market funds, you can take a look at the PowerShare Dynamic Europe (PEH), the iShares S&P Europe 350 (IEV), the iShares MSCI Japan (EWJ), the iShares MSCI Australia (EWA), and iSHares MSCI Canada (EWC).

Accessing Emerging Markets

If you would like to get into emerging markets, then do so using all-encompassing ETFs. A good one is the iShares Emerging Markets Index (EEM). This one will give you exposure to such countries like Taiwan, Brazil, South Africa, South Korea, China, Turkey, Hungary, and Israel.

Perhaps you would much rather target a specific region. In that case, your best bet is the WisdomTree Middle East Dividend (GULF), PowerShares MENA Frontier Countries (PMNA), SPDR S&P EMerging Europe (GUR), or you could go for SPDR S&P Emerging Asia Pacific (GMF). By the way, SPDR is pronounced "spider."

If your focus is on BRICs, then you'll be pleased to know that there are a handful of ETFs you can get involved in. There is the SPDR S&P BRIC (BIK), the Claymore/BNY BRIC (EEB, and the iShares MSCI BRIC (BKF).

Choosing Your Funds

If you're going to select a fund, you have got to take a peek beneath the hood, so you can see what country has what weighting. Say you're interested in China more than anything else. You could go for BIK, since it gives China a weighting of 42.8 percent. If you're more into Brazil, you could go for the EEB, with a 49.4 percent weighting for Brazil.

If you're more interested in the emerging market of a particular country, then there are funds which will allow you to invest in that market. You've got Market Vectors Russia (RSX), iShares MSCI Israel (EIS), Market Vectors Indonesia (IDX), and iShares MSCI Thailand (THD) among others. Just let your fingers do some Googling, before you part with your money.

CHAPTER SEVEN

Yummy Sectors

At the moment, the doors are wide open to you. There are a lot of sectors just waiting, begging for you to invest in them. The way the market is set up right now will give you more chances than ever before to grow your portfolio to unimaginable heights. There are some people who do not approve of the way the market has been split up recently, but the fact is this is a good thing, because it gives you so many options. With the right options, you have room to grow. Also, the way the market is set up allows for healthy competition, and that fosters widespread growth. It's a great time to be alive. It's a great time to be an investor.

It doesn't matter that one market is down, or another is barely even moving. You are sure to find something you can ride high to profits. When it comes to subsectors, you can find them telling a different story in trends compared to the larger markets. This means no matter the state the market is in, you can make money. Another thing I should tell you about subsectors is that the room for profit is beyond enough, whether you're talking about the economic warriors, the emerging countries, currencies, commodities, utilities, telecoms, transport, and more! The market has got so many components to it, and each of these components react in different ways compared to the whole, and other components. Some of them move in lockstep, while others are opposed to one another.

Boom and bust is a reality in every market, and economy. The US economy is not exempt from this reality. If you want a reminder, recall the era of tech investments. That said, you have certain companies that move along on their own way, regardless of what else is happening around them. While the power grid may not be doing so great, that does not affect what's happening in the healthcare sector. Or when things are going south with Big Pharma, things could be looking good for the power sector as a new power source is developed that is a lot more efficient than anything we've ever known.

The economy in America is made up of so many different parts. You've got the media, finance, aviation, transportation, aerospace, healthcare, defense, engineering, and others. As an investor, you have the option of niching down even further to get at sub sectors like biotech, pharmaceuticals, regional banks, renewable energy, and so on.

Thanks to ETFs, you can have your pick of them all. All you have to do is determine out how specific you want to get with your investments. You could choose a broad sector if you're going for stability, or if you like the volatility and the idea of high rewards, you could look into niching down your investments.

Cyclical Investing

There are certain sectors and companies that do pretty well during certain market phases. Steel, fine dining, and automobile companies do great when the economy booms, but as soon as things start to go south with the broader economy, things go south with these sectors as well. This is the mechanism behind cyclical investing.

There are some investors who have learned to exploit cyclical investing to their advantage, and make a killing with it. As far as I am concerned though, I believe that trend following remains the superior way to go, and my portfolio and clients can attest to that fact. With trend following, there is no need to try to predict the beginning and end of cycles. It's strictly about what the price action and the 200-day exponential moving average tell you, nothing more, and nothing less.

Technologic

The past twenty years have been amazing for technology. Looking back, it's almost difficult to describe how far tech has gone. Your cell phone has a bajillion times more computing power than the computers that were used back in the day, which had to take up entire rooms! It's crazy how far the tech has come. That said, with all the growth that has been experienced by the technological sub sector, there have been some bad times as well. Yes, I'm talking about the 90s.

When the internet was created, the US military could never have predicted just how popular it was going to get. Come 1995, everything changed. Up to 18 million people were online. Speculators noticed, and they wanted in on that action. The internet was a valuable piece of tech, and it looked like it would remain that way. So, everyone began to invest in technology.

Next thing you know you're hearing about how Billy just became a millionaire the other day, and the day before that it was Louise, whose investment in tech had paid off. People were getting options, eager to get into tech one way or another. Just as the bubble was peaking, it was ridiculously easy for a random, brand new IT company to have an IPO and raise mad money from it, regardless of whether it was actually doing anything productive or not.

This made investors all the more eager to get in on the action. They didn't think much about the real story being told by these companies' balance sheets. They just bought up as much of the stocks as they could, believing the lie that profits were inevitable in the future. The one fundamental they should have looked at was completely ignored. If they had bothered to look, they would not have crashed and burned so hard.

Everyone was overtaken by greed, and there was a tech buying mania. It didn't matter what they were buying, as long as it had a dotcom attached to it, they were sold. Come October 1990, the NASDAQ Index hit a low of 300, mostly burdened by tech. Come March 2000, it hit a little over 5000. That was a whopping 1456 percent increase. While the improvements in tech continued to flood in, and productivity soared, profits remained where they were.

Pop! Goes the Bubble

For years, the tech mania went on and one. Eventually, the first signs of trouble showed up, as companies reported losses of enormous proportions, and began to go belly up, just months after they had their IPOs. 1999 alone saw 457 IPOs, which were mostly tied to tech and the internet. On the first day of trading, 117 of those doubled in price. From March 10, 2000, to October 9, 2002, the NASDAQ Composite dropped by a whopping 78 percent, as price went from 5,048 to 1,114. And then of course, the blame game began. Some people say it was because there was too much happening too fast that the dotcom era was a bust, and that companies were expected to deliver too much, too soon, when they hadn't even figured out what direction they wanted to go in tech.

While people were investing money in tech, the Vanguard 500 S&P 500 fund was booming. It had, for the first time since its inception, a lot more in outflows, come March 2000. This was just as the NASDAQ had peaked at 5048, it's 52-week high.

Those who bought into tech companies suffered for it — especially those who bought right at the top and never got out. In 2019, they still would not be able to recoup their losses. This is why you don't buy and hold. Now, I'm not saying there's anything wrong with joining a trend — after all, this is the strategy that I have shared with you. However, you must have an exit strategy. A lot of these folks did not have one in place, and they lost big time because of that. Whether it's Bitcoin, or some other new-fangled thing that comes around, know this: There's always a bubble, and sooner or later, it's always going to pop. Don't listen to anyone who tells you, "But this is different! There's nothing like it!" When you hear that, remember the 90s. Remember Bitcoin. That went from about $20,000 down to $3,000. Remember that, and you'll spare yourself headaches, heartaches, and heart attacks. Also, don't listen to the folks who say it will come back up. It's been over a decade, and the NASDAQ hasn't even approached the old highs of 2000.

EFTs Tied to Specific Sectors

When you invest in sector-specific EFTs, you will basically be investing in a group of companies that are all in one specific sector. This is a much better option than choosing a single stock that could at best give you profits, or more likely than not, cause you to lose.

Keep in mind that each sector has got hundreds of companies. What are the odds that you will choose the right one? It's much better to just focus on the sector as a whole. That way, you can have as many as 100 of them, making your chances for profits better. There is no guarantee that you will find the next Facebook, so don't count on that.

These days, EFTs are becoming more and more specialized, leaving it completely up to your discretion how narrow you would like to go. For instance, there is the broad sector of healthcare. You could decide to niche down by focusing on companies involved in nanotech for health, or gene modification or something of the sort. The transportation sector is broad, but you can niche down by focusing on companies involved in railway transport and airlines. This is the same logic that applies to all sectors and sub sectors.

If you do not find it easy to come to decisions, sector ETFs could be for you. If you want to invest in a sector that you believe in for one reason or the other, you could niche down. There is nothing stopping you from mixing and matching as you please. Do remember though, that the narrower you go, the more likely you will have volatility, which means increased risk, as well as an increased likelihood of being profitable. If you want to limit your risk, then you've got to increase your exposure by choosing a broader sector ETF.

Other Sectors to Invest In

What follows is a list of sectors you can invest in, not just in the United States, but the rest of the world as well.

Utility ETFs

These are great for investors, especially because there are tax rules which would favor those who receive dividends from utilities ETFs. To sum it up, you will get taxed at a rate of 15 percent, rather than the regular percentage you would have to pay for income taxes. You can choose a bunch of utilities, if you're into them. Some good ones to consider are the Rydex S&P Equal Weight Utilities ETF (RYU), the Utilities Select SPDR (XLU), and the Vanguard Utilities ETF (VPU).

Banking

Since 2008, people have been a bit more cautious with this sector. That said, there are still those who get benefits from investing in this sector. You'll find that the Select Sector SPDR Financial (XLF) happens to be a crowd pleaser, as it has the collective stocks of over 80 of the United States' largest, finest financial institutions, and is traded quite heavily, day in and day out. A few other ETFs to think about are the iShares Dow Jones U.S. Financial Services (IYG), the Rydex S&P Equal Weight Financials (RYF), the iShares S&P Global Financials (IXG), and the KBW Regional Banking (KRE).

Healthcare ETFs

People who opt for healthcare ETFs do this so that they can hopefully get some much-needed reforms in the health sector. Some of the ones you could get into are the Health Care Select Sector SPDR (XLV), the iShares Dow Jones U.S. Health Care (IYH), and the Rydex S&P Equal Weight Health Care ETF (RYH).

CHAPTER EIGHT

Gold and Black Gold

It's funny that during the techno mania of the 1990s, no one really gave a rip about gold, which was and continues to be one of the safest possible investments you could make that would give you a lot of bang for your buck. The funny thing is banks couldn't get rid of their gold fast enough as at June 1999, because it was thought that gold would no longer have any value. For this reason, come June 21, 1999, gold sank to an incredible low of $252.90 per ounce. That would have been a steal if you had bought then.

It didn't take long for the depression to lift, especially after the 9/11 attacks. Since then, gold has been on a steady uptrend since 2001.

Why Gold is Golden

There's a reason investors love gold. There's a reason it became the safe haven commodity when things get rough and tough. It's not just about the fact that it looks good to have gold wristwatches and gold toilets. It's that gold really does its uses in the industrial sector, too. It's not really about getting all decked in gold, for investors.

Investors are of the opinion that gold is real money. This has been the wide held opinion, all over the world. Sure, there are other commodities that have appreciable value, but they are not gold. Gold. Up until 1971, the price of gold was set at $35 per troy ounce. This price was the gold standard, but that ended when the US decided to stop allowing dollars to be directly converted to gold. Since the dollar was taken off the gold standard, this meant that the price of gold could fly, or die.

So, till date, investors are still very much about their gold, because they love nothing more than taking advantage of the rising price of gold, and they also love that it serves as a great, safe haven for tough times. Historically, gold has always remained valuable, no matter how bad things get. This means no matter how volatile the markets are, or how badly things sink, gold will always be of some value. People value assets that are real over assets that are only paper. When the markets crashed in 2008, gold soared on, like nothing was going on.

From January 2000 to March 2008, gold has steadily moved upward. Even now it continues to surge. Now a word of advice: Gold is incredibly volatile, and you need to be cautious with it. I've seen it move thousands of points in a matter of hours, so it would pay you well to be on the right side of the trade. It's also subject to a lot of whipsawing, but the truth is you can make money, if you're smart about your risks, and smart about following the trend. There's one other form of gold that has always matched the price of yellow gold as you know it. We will look at that now.

Black Gold

I'm talking about oil. It's slippery, but it's got the ability to make your portfolio merrily obese, just like yellow gold. Usually, oil and gold tend to be highly correlated, meaning they move in tandem.

Oil matters. Until we figure out other renewable energy sources and have them in place globally, it will continue to matter. It is important. It's not called black gold for nothing. A lot of economies are heavily dependent on oil. This same oil has made a lot of people wealthier than you could probably imagine. Since it's finite, that just means that oil is going to remain of much value to us all. Even as supplies dwindle, the price continues to climb.

Without oil, you could not heat your home, you couldn't make plastic, and you couldn't possibly run your car, unless you've got an electric one. Unless that electric car is charged by solar, you still kinda need oil to have your electricity. Any company that's in the ol sector right now is sure to be raking in made money. It helps that the world demands more and more oil every day.

Investors recognize that oil is valuable, and that is why they want in on this. The fact that it's filthy and slippery is not a deterrent. Oil is an asset, and it always rises during times of inflation, and when there's scarcity and demand is high. If you've got oil under your feet right now, you have no idea how wealthy you could potentially be! But you've got to set up a rig and stuff, and I don't know about you, but that is way too much trouble. Just because you can't get a rig doesn't mean you can't get a piece of the oily, slippery pie.

It's a tad tricky to invest in oil, for a lot of reasons, because a lot of factors can affect the cost of oil at a moment's notice. The politics around oil can be very complex, oil producing countries have policies that control the price and supply of oil, and they could take decisions at any point that would make the market too volatile, even the weather could affect the production of oil.

The fact of the matter is you can make a killing with oil... Or it can kill your portfolio, if you're not smart about it. The way to be smart about it is already in your head. What is it? Following the trend, using a stop loss, using your exits when you should.

Trends Equal Profits

No one has any idea where gold or oil will go. The best you can do is to just follow the trend. No one knows where the price is going to go. I don't care what they say, there is no way to predict the price of any commodity, ETF, fund, or any other financial product, so don't let anyone sell you some scammy auto trader or account management service. And really, forget about fundamentals, except when you need them to let you know if you should stay away from a trade for a bit, until things quiet down, like after news releases. Don't marry your positions. If the trend says it's the other way around compared to the position you're in, do a 180. The one time you do not need to stick to your guns is when you're investing.

Don't give in to the tendency to want to predict things and

be right. That's gambling, and that's not what this is about. You're trading and investing to make money, and keep it. You'll notice that there are a lot of traders and investors who just love to predict. They love to draw stuff on their chart and tell you just what price is going to do at every level. It seems like they are oh so knowledgeable. You wish you had that inner crystal ball you could gaze in so that you, too, could **just know** that gold is going to go back to one dollar at some point in the future. Don't wish for that. These guys know nothing. No one owns the market. It goes where it will. The only thing you can do is follow it.

Your Own Commodities

Commodities are seen to be in a different class of assets altogether. They are known for being really volatile. That said, they do not necessarily reflect the true picture of what's going on in the global stock markets. They have their own trends. Since they are available to be traded as ETFs, you can also add them to your portfolio to make you even more money.

You have the option of going with futures, a basket of stocks made up of commodity producers, or physical commodities. It wasn't always like this. You couldn't play in this game, back then. It was only the big boys and sharks and whales that could swim in that ocean. Thanks to ETFs, it's a lot more affordable for the average Jane and Joe to get involved in black gold and yellow gold.

Types of Commodity ETFs

You've got the physical commodities. This is basically

like straight up owning the commodity itself, by buying it directly. However, it's not a practical way to do things. What you can do instead is simply buy an ETF that has oil or gold in the mix. This way, you have actual shares that give you part ownership of these commodities.

Another type of commodity ETF are the individual commodity futures. These are affected by the underlying commodity's spot price. By spot price, I mean the present price of the commodity. So, when the price changes, your future contracts will also change in value. One goes up, so does the other. Do keep in mind though that if you make any money, or even lose any, your profits and losses will be taxed annually, to the tune of 60 percent for long term gains, and 40 percent for short term gains, no matter how long you held on to the positions.

Next, you've got Commodity indexes. With ETFs that are connected to commodity indexes, you have the option of diversifying your assets, mixing it up so you have broad ETFs as well as special sector ones.

Finally, you've got commodity equities. These will allow you to have a basket of various companies that are in charge of processing or creating a commodity. Unlike commodities futures, there is an entirely different risk/reward profile here, since if you invest, you will be exposed to risk that would affect the company, as well as risk that affects the commodity itself. This is both good and bad. It's great when you reap the rewards of company stocks that continue to climb, but if both the company and commodity take a beating, then so will your portfolio. The choice is up to you, to decide the way you would like to expose yourself to commodities. It's all down to how comfortable you are with the risk you'll be dealing with.

Agriculture

Land and energy have both gone up in price, and have steadily risen over time. Land is going to become even more valuable, as we continue to have more and more babies. We will need more land not just to live on, but to love off, as well. So, it makes sense to invest in agricultural commodities. Great ones are soybeans, coffee, sugar, cattle, cotton, hogs, corn, and wheat, among others. Here are some ETFs you should look into, for agriculture: Market Vector Global Agribusiness (MOO), and PowerShares DB Agriculture (DBA).

Metals

For metals, we must take a look at all three: Base, precious, as well as industrial metals. You've got copper, platinum, silver, gold, palladium, and steel. These are used in construction, for industrial work, and as jewelry as well. With metals, the price action is often affected by economic as well as geopolitical issues in the countries that are dominant producers of metal (Australia, the US, and South Africa) as well as the dominant consumers (the US, and India). That said, each one still has certain unique attributes in terms of fundamentals. To get into metals, look into PowerShares DB Gold Fund (DGL), Market Vectors Steel (SLX), SPDR Gold Shares Fund (GLD), iShares COMEX Gold Trust (AU), iShares Silver Trust (SLV) and PowerShares DB Base Metals (DBB).

Energy

Energy is key. This is how the world is run, and that is not going to change any time soon. The demand for energy will continue to grow by leaps and bounds, and so it only makes sense to add it to your ETF portfolio. The truth is that India, China, and other emerging markets will keep on building lots and lots of factories, and this will mean that they will have an increased need for energy. Even as their populations continue to grow rapidly, so will the need for energy. Today's world is mostly fueled by oil and gas. Renewable forms of energy are being eagerly worked on as well. Energy will always be in demand, and the fact that oil and gas are finite, means that they will always be valuable. These commodities can be affected by political unrest, as well as the weather, among other things, so keep in mind that they are incredibly volatile, so keep your eye on the trend, and only follow that. If you want to get involved in energy, take a look at PowerShares DB Energy Fund (DBE), United States Oil Fund (USO), iShares Dow Jones U.S. Energy Sector Index Fund (IYE), and United States Gasoline (UGA).

Broad Based Commodity ETFs

If you can't quite figure out what to go for, then you might want to consider going for the broad-based commodity ETFs. Consider the PowerShares DB Commodity Index Tracking Fund (DBC), and the iShares S&P GSCI Commodity Indexed Trust (GSG).

Blending Countries and Commodities

If you cannot settle on a commodity, or figure out which country you'd be interested in exposing your portfolio to, then you might as well look into getting ETFs of countries that are abundant in natural resources as well as commodities. There are a lot of countries like this and you should be able to get involved in their ETF market this way.

The reason you should consider getting single-country funds is that these funds will let you have some exposure to commodities, and at the same time, you will have the option of further diversifying your portfolio, which you would miss out on if you were to go for a single commodity fund. Keep in mind that there are some funds that are quite heavily weighted in commodities. This means the country's economies might depend on them a little too much. A good example would be Russia. You have a lot of options, but consider the following:

Russia, has been doing incredibly well in finance since 2000. However, the trends have been going down since the end of 2008, and right now their banks have to deal with liquidity issues. The economy relies a lot on raw materials as well as energy. Be mindful of the exchange rates, as well as the corruption. You can get into Russia's markets by checking out the Market Vectors Russia ETF (RSX).

Chile has an economy that is amenable to foreign trade, and it also has healthy finances. You will notice that about 75 percent of Chile's exports are made up of commodities. Chile is dependent on its copper, and that alone makes up 33 percent of the country's revenue. The government there has a fiscal policy that is counter-cyclical, holding on to wealth gotten from surpluses in trade in times of economic boom, and then falling back on deficit spending when times are down. To get into Chile and copper, consider iShares MSCI Chile Investable Market Index (ECH).

South Africa is responsible for most of the world's chromium, platinum, and gold. The country is also an emerging market, and it boasts of a very large middle class. They've got developed legal, communications, transport, financial, and energy systems. However, there is a lot of joblessness, and the infrastructure in place does not quite allow for growth. The government does what it can to prevent inflation, and create budget surpluses and jobs making use of enterprises it owns. You can get into South Africa using the iShares MSCI South Africa Index (EZA).

Australia happens to be the top exporter of coal in the world, with a high per capita GDP. Its government is all about reforms, keeping inflation low, improving the housing market, and creating better ties with China, in trade. To get involved in Australian commodity ETFs, check out iShares MSCI Australia Index (EWA).

It's really a neat thing to add commodities to your ETF portfolio, as they tend to move in the opposite direction of whatever affects stocks. In a way, this could keep you hedged at best, or making money regardless of what is going on. Also, stocks can decline in value over time, and can even be gotten rid of for not performing, meaning you can no longer trade them, and whoever is still trading them at that point would suffer loss Commodities are good to have because they can take the sting out of that if it happens, and they will always be of value, regardless of the fluctuations that are inevitable and dependent on the growth of the world's economies

CHAPTER NINE

Fixed Income

For the most part, people do not really think about bonds when things are good, especially because bonds are seen as conservative, and what fun is conservative when you're trying to get rich quick? However, it would behoove you to take a look at the bonds market as well. When it comes to risk versus reward, the bond market would look pretty good in your portfolio.

One thing about the bonds market is that it has its very own trends. They range from very conservative, to very aggressive — meaning from little risk, to great risk. When it comes to risk in the bonds market, you have to deal with the standard deviation measurement of the classic return volatility. You also have to think about the fact that bonds are risky in terms of interest rates, and constantly react as the rates change. If you're working with bonds that have a longer maturity, then those will be even more susceptible to the changes in interest rates. Keeping this in mind, you could determine the level of risk you're willing to expose your portfolio to, and size the assets in your portfolio accordingly.

Type of Bonds

You've got the US Treasury Bonds, which are the safest place for you to park your money. The reason I say this is that the United States of America is a very stable country, and you're not likely to hear about it defaulting when it comes to debts. The thing to keep in mind here is that while it is really safe, the tradeoff is that the yields are pretty low. There was once a time when the yields were even negative. What that meant was that the people of the United States were basically paying the government at the time to hold on to their hard-earned cash.

Next up, you've got corporate bonds, which are a bit on the riskier side, since it is not unusual for corporations to fail to pay their debts. Since there is a fair bit of risk, there is also a fair bit of reward as well, so they could well be worth it if you've got an aggressive risk appetite.

Municipal bonds are another type you should look into. These are bonds that are given out by localities and states. If you want safety, then keep in mind they are nowhere near as safe as treasury bonds are. They are safe, but only to a certain point. It is a rare case when a municipality, or state or locality is hit by bankruptcy, since they can simply get more revenue by taxing the citizens, but it does happen every now and again. The one good thing about municipal bonds though, is that you do not have to worry about paying federal taxes.

Junk bonds are bonds that are usually thought of as being high yield. I should not have to point out that they are incredibly risky. They are in fact the riskiest place for you to sink your money into. You may have heard of high yield debt.

These are basically the same as junk bonds. However, if you've got the stomach for it, you can get in on this too, as they pay very handsome rewards, when they do pan out.

Finally, you've got foreign bonds. There is no reason you should not look outside of the US to get involved in the bonds market. There are foreign corporations, municipalities, and governments who will also issue debt in their various currencies. Not unlike in the US bond market, there are variations in risk. The key risk to keep in mind involved that of the currency, as when the interest rates change, you might have to deal with some loss.

Beware the Bubble

The bonds market is not exempt from bubbles either, so keep that in mind. One of the recent ones was in 2008 to 2009. The belief that the bubble was about to pop caused a lot of people to move over to treasuries instead. There is one thing you should always keep an eye out for, when bubbles pop: The chance to buy cheap, and then ride the trend to newer, greater heights. You can make sure you're always on the right side of things, by making use of the 200-exponential moving average strategy which I have shared with you earlier on in this book.

Why Invest in Bonds?

You really should get into the bonds market, because they are versatile beyond compare, and are some of the best investment vehicles you could ever hope to use. With bonds, you can actually boost your capital by making use of high yield returns. Just make sure you do your homework, so that you're not caught off guard because you were not aware of the inherent risks.

Another great reason to get involved in bonds is that they are absolutely fantastic for diversification. They will help you make sure that the risk that you'll have in your portfolio is properly spread about, so that at worst, you're at break even, and at best, you are constantly growing your portfolio.

Bonds can be a great way for you to protect your capital, while you reap from the interest, giving you an extra source of income that you have instant access to. With bonds, you can keep your savings truly safe, especially if you know you've got some big spends to make in the not too distant future. All you've got to do is set the maturity date of your bonds to match those times when you will need them.

Age

You need to keep in mind when you will need to be able to tap into your funds, as well as the risk you're willing to accept. If you're 80, your needs and risk appetite are going to be far different from that of a 30-year-old.

When you're in your 20s, up to your 30s, what you're thinking about is how to make money. So, for you your risk appetite can be a bit high, ranging on down to moderate. So, chances are bonds will not be a huge part of your portfolio right now.

When you hit your 40s, and move on through your 50s, you'll find your appetite for risk is dropping, and you're only willing to expose your portfolio to bonds which are safe, moving away from the riskier stuff like corporate and junk bonds.

Once you hit your 60s, and move on from there, chances are you're going to retire, or you've already done so. All that will matter to you is that you have a portfolio that allows you to live off of it, and you want to keep it safe. What the experts say is when you hit this point, you should consider allocating at least 50 percent of your portfolio to bonds.

Other Things to Consider

The thing about bonds is that they are tricky. If you're going to invest, you need to remember a few things: the higher the prices of bonds go, the more likely their yield will drop. When there is a lot of demand, when investors are looking for safer pastures to park their green in, then there's the likelihood for the price to rice, when it comes to treasury bonds, while the yields decline. When the price of corporate bonds go down, the yields go up as well.

Keep in mind as well that you need to be aware of the quality of the credit, so you can figure out whether or not the quality of the investment is good enough for you. It's the rating that helps you understand whether or not a bond is actually credit worth, as well as what the default risk is, exactly. Often, these ratings are issued by a ratings service, like Moody's, or Standard and Poor's. With these ratings, you can tell just how strong or weak the issuer of the bond is. Basically, it's to let you know whether or not the issuer can pay the interest in full, and on time. The quality of the credit happens to change as time goes by, and it tends to go down when things are bad in the markets.

Standard and Poor's Ratings

Here are the S&P ratings, so you know what you're looking for:

- AAA and AA mean the bonds are of high credit quality.
- AA and BBB mean the bonds are of medium credit quality.
- BB, B, CCC, and C, means that the bonds are of low credit quality. These are the ratings for junk bonds.
- D is the rating for bonds that are in default.

When we talk about yield, we refer to what the income returns are on an investment. It's often stated as an annual percentage. With bonds, you've got four different kinds of yields.

- Coupon, which means that the interest rate of the bond has been fixed upon issuance.
- Current yield, which is basically the return you earn annually on the price you pay for the bond.
- Yield to maturity refers to the sum of returns that you'll receive as an investor, when you hold on to the bond until it is mature. The interests accrue from the day you buy the bonds, to the day they mature. This also includes the interest that accrues on the interests. You've also got the appreciation and depreciation of the price of the bond factored in as well.
- Ta equivalent refers to municipally bonds that are not taxable. They will always have a tax equivalent yield. This tax equivalent yield is largely determined by your

tax bracket as an investor.

With bonds, you have to be very aware of the interest rate risks that are unavoidable. The relationship between bonds and interest rates is inverse in nature. A rise in interest rates means that bond prices will drop, and vice versa as well. This is not random. The reason this happens is that investors are very interested in locking in the bonds at the highest rates that they can get, and to hold on to them for as long as they can. So, they're always on the lookout for bonds that will pay a much better rate than the current rate of the market. This causes demand to surge, which also causes the price to go up, and the interest rates to go down. So, something you should keep in mind is that if the bond has a shorter maturity than others, then it is less likely to be hit by a rise in interest rates. If you've got bonds in times of low yields and minimal inflation, however, then you would be better off going for the long-term bonds, if you want the best gains you can get.

What the Yield Curve Is

The yield curve matters, as it acts as an indicator of what's going on in the economy. It helps you see where other investors think the economy is going to go. With the yield curve, you see the interest rates of bonds that have equal credit quality, but different dates of maturity plotted within a set time frame. This is how you're able to tell what changes are happening in the economy, in terms of productivity and growth.

It's basically a line graph that shows you the connection between the time of bonds maturity for an asset class and credit quality, as well as the yields to maturity. The line will often start from the spot interest rate, and move on out over a period of 30 years.

Thanks to the yield curve, you can see what differences in yield exist on account of a difference in maturity. You can also see what the whole picture is like at any point in time, when it comes to the market, maturities, and rates. It shows you that the longer the maturity is, the more the yields from the bonds are.

You can make use of the yield curve to set up your portfolio, by looking out for bonds that seem cheap or pricey at any point in time. You can then see how much you're likely to get over a set period of time.

When you have a steep yield curve, what it means is that the long-term rates are much higher than the short-term rates, and so you should opt for long term maturation periods. When the yield curve is flat, that means you need to avoid investing, because the risk remains the same at all maturation periods, and there is not much in the way of yields. When there is an inverted yield curve, then you've got the long rates offering less value than the short rates.

Trends Lately

Back in 20087, the bonds market was crazy with volatility, and so a lot of investors got interested in the fixed income markets. Treasury yields were incredibly low, lower than ever. Only a few investors took a moment to think about whether or not it was worth holding on to a 30-year bond, only to receive 3 percent to 4 percent, or even treasury bills with a negative yield. At this time, funny enough, corporate bond yields were doing exceptionally well, some of them giving yields of over 10 percent, others up to 20 percent. While corporate bonds funds as well as ETFs would decline, the yields would go up in value.

If you believe there is a chance for things to pick up again, you have a few routes you could go down. First, you could choose not to take ownership of single bonds, unless you intend to hold on to them until they mature. You could make sure that you have a sell point for the ETFs and bonds funds, making use of the 200-period exponential moving average on the daily timeframe. You could also pick out those ETFs that are proving a lot more sensitive to rising rates than usual, in advance. I'm talking about long maturity funds here.

Trends in Municipal Bonds and Taxes

One more thing that is trending is tax. On account of the recession, both state and federal governments had to shoulder a lot of burden, especially when it comes to the budgets. In order to fix this, taxes have continued to go up, particularly for the wealthier investors. You can take advantage of this up trend in taxes by making use of the tax-exempt bond market. The thing about the yields in the tax-exempt bond market is that they are not taxed federally, and they continue to increase in value as taxes keep rising. If the bond happens to serve on a state level, then that means you do not have to pay taxes on both the federal level, and the state level as well.

Enter municipal bond funds, which are a part of the EF market. This segment has been growing by leaps and bounds.

Now, you're not going to get returns that will knock your socks off, but you'll like these because they are tax free on a federal level, and on a state level if it so happens that you purchase bonds from your state. What really makes them attractive is the taxable equivalent yield, when you do the math.

Before you can really figure out and compare the tax-exempt yields available, you need to calculate the taxable equivalent yield, also known as the TEY. What the TEY does is help you understand the taxable return you must get before you can equate that to a certain tax-exempt yield, while considering the tax bracket you fall into. The easiest way to work this out is to divide the tax-exempt yield by one, subtracted from your federal tax bracket. The resulting percentage is what you must get in terms of taxable investments, as it relates to the percentage of the municipal investment. Before you ask, no, possible upgrades in municipal bonds over corporate bonds are not factored in here.

The great thing about municipal ETFs is that the fees are little. It's never more than half of what you would be charged with a municipal bond fund, and that means you get to save a lot of money. Where government funds are very liquid, there are times when municipal bonds have episodes of being illiquid, especially when there is volatility in price. This was in the case in 2007 and 2008. That still provides you some opportunity as an investor to get in on yields that are high exempt, if you're planning to invest for the long haul.

If you find it difficult to settle on going tax-free versus taxable when you're investing in bonds, then you can take advantage of calculators like the one at the investing Bonds website. You could also contact an accountant, to help you understand this better

Opportunities for High Yield

The market's bubble may have burst back in the 1990s, but that set the stage for long term profits. Then in 2007 and 2008, there was more and more fear surrounding the rise of default rates. At this point, returns went as high as 20 percent. That said, there is a chance that as the economy bounces back over time, the companies which are being speculated upon should become more of a honeypot for investors to park their funds in. You could get the kinds of returns the equity market would give you. Thanks to ETFs, you have an easy, and liquid way to access this particularly volatile market.

Fixed Income ETFs: Worth It

Just before 2007, the fixed income ETFs as a market was really restricted. You had to be okay with simply keeping track of well-known indexes like the NASDAQ and S&P 500, before getting in on the relatively new kinds of ETFs that were set up to track currency, commodities, and then bonds. More often than not though, people make use of ETFs to make investments in the stock market.

iShares happens to be the first provider that made it possible for you and I as investors to be able to play in the bond market using ETFs. Over time, iShares continued to grow and expand, giving us more and more funds to invest in. in less than a couple of years, the world of the fixed income ETFs had doubled. Other competitors are not blind to this, and there are more ETF providers who keep adding brand new funds to their available options. ETF providers offer fixed income ETFs as one more way for you to invest in ETFs.

There are three major things to keep in mind when it comes to indexed bond ETFs. First of all, the costs are ridiculously low. The ratio of expenses for bond ETFs are frequently between 0.15 and 0.2 percent. It just depends on things like maturities, and credits in the bond index. However, the more your bond ETF is specialized, the more the expense ratio will be. It's not illogical, since the more you niche down, the more you need to keep it up. Also, there are all sorts of individual bonds that you can only buy in increments of $5,000, which means it is not at all easy to get access to individual bonds cheaply, and easily.

Furthermore, you might have to pay for additional costs of trading. Not unlike mutual funds, the expense ratio of the annual ETF will not include the trading costs that can quickly pile up. Your account and portfolio are not being managed for free either. While the transaction fees are as little as to seem insignificant, the fact is that over a bunch of trades, they can really add up. So, you've got to set it up right so that the costs will not eat into your returns.

Finally, distributions ideally had better be mostly interest income. When you take a look at the iShares Aggregate Bond (AGG), and the iShares Broad Based Indexed Bond ETF, paying particular attention to their distribution history, you will notice that there has not been any distribution at all of long term or short-term capital gains. What does get distributed is the interest. Before you get overly excited, you need to know this does not necessarily mean that in the future, capital gains will not be distributed. However, the fact remains that when it comes to the indexed bond ETFs, the distributions are based on interest, and not capital gains.

Do You Need Bonds?

A lot of investors in the bonds market are in it indefinitely. So, it helps to add bonds to your portfolio if you're looking to retire rich, or you have events in the future you know will require a fair bit of spending on your part. Bonds are safe, for the most part, and if you invest in them wisely, you won't have to worry about costs. Something that is typically done is to use this formula: Take your current age, and then subtract it from 100. The result is the percentage that you should allocate to stocks, while the rest of it should go towards bonds.

Keep in mind also that just like bonds, bond ETFs have varying styles and risk appetites. Say you want broad exposure ETF bonds. With broad exposure, these are typically the yardstick for measuring the bond market of the US investment grade. If you want a cheap way to get in on this action, then you can check out the Vanguard Total Bond Market (BND), which keeps track of the Barclays Capital US Aggregate Bond Index.

If you're looking for short term ETF bonds, that's great, as they will help you to be cautious about rises in interest rates which are indeed a possibility. You could opt for the iShares MBS Bond Fund (MBB), which keeps track of the Barclays

Capital US MBS Fixed Rate Index.

Want to go with municipal bond ETFs? Then you should go with the iShares S&P National Municipal Bond (MUB) which keeps track of the S&P National Municipal Bond Index.

Should you choose corporate bond ETFs, then you want to try the iShares iBoxx $ Investment Grade Corporate Bond (LQD), which keeps track of the iBoxx $ Liquid Investment Grade Index.

If you're more into high yield bond ETFs, then you can check out the PowerShares High Yield Corporate Bond (PHB).

Choosing Your Bond ETFs

When you opt for purchasing an ETF which keeps track of a bond index, it's just easier, and will cost you a lot less than buying bonds on their own. It's really as easy as one transaction. Just like with all other financial products, you have options. You can decide how broad you want to be with your investments. You could choose to niche down. You could select any of the bond funds I've mentioned before, or you could simply sink your money into any of the ETFs in the total bond market.

Bond ETFs offer you a lot of security, as long as you do your due diligence and are well aware and respectful of the attendant risks, which we have discussed already. The advantage of bond ETFs is that they allow you to really diversify your portfolio, and they really are your best when investing in the bonds market. In addition to the diversification you can get, you also will enjoy liquidity, since the ETF is publicly traded

On an exchange that is visible to all, rather than traded using an underwriter. With bond ETFs, you will get all the exposure you'd like to the market, with some risk, but you will also be generously rewarded if you play smart. If you're very interested in flexible trading, and if transparency matters to you, then you definitely should get involved in the bond ETF market. It's easy for you to see what is really going on with your portfolio, any day, any time. All you need is to go online. Compare that to an index bond mutual fund, which will only give you that information maybe twice a year, and you can see why bond ETFs are just so much more attractive.

If you're concerned about liquidity, bond ETFs make use of a little something known as representative sampling. What this means is that the funds will only ever keep track of enough bonds that will paint a picture of what the whole index looks like. Usually, the bonds that are monitored happen to be the most liquid and the largest of the lot. For instance, you've got the Lehman Aggregate Bond Index with over 6000 bonds. However, the Barclays iShares Lehman Aggregate Bond Fund (AGG) has its focus on just a little over a hundred of these sample bonds.

CHAPTER TEN

LEVERAGE

It's not unusual for investors to decide to go short in bear markets. Some people only prefer to be long, while there are those who want to make money in both bull runs and bear scenarios. You have the option of selling stocks you do not actually own, if you believe that a company is about to take a hit, or you can see judging from the 200-period exponential moving average that it is time to go short. The way this works is when you decide to sell these shares that you do not actually own, your broker will borrow them from a different client, and then lend them to you. As you make your money, you get to keep it, as long as you pay the commission owed to your brokers.

When you short stocks, you can make money, even if the stock is losing value. This is why I am not part of the buy and hold team. The goal is to make money, and while we may have altruistic notions of wanting every company out there to do well, we cannot let those get in the way of having a more robust portfolio in bear markets.

Going short has its advantages. It's a great way to stay

hedged and protected, especially in times of uncertainty in the market, or during pull backs, when you do not intend to liquidate your buys.

ETFs: Long, and Short

Both short and long ETFs have been around for a while, but they really begin to pick up steam in 2008. At the time, the stock market was doing poorly, and had been performing this way since 1931. There were a lot of investors who did not want to simply cash out and then wait for things to begin moving back up again. So, what they did instead was to invest in leveraged and inverse ETFs, causing the assets in this market to climb, and putting some money in their pockets even as things kept getting worse.

With leveraged ETFs, you have the option of going long or short in the market several times. Now, it is best to go with the trend following strategy when you're working with the classic ETFs. That said, you can also use the trend following strategy to get some more juice out of the market both up and down. You just have to keep your eyes on those funds.

Short ETFs, also known as inverse ETFs, make use of derivatives to make money off of a reduction in the value of the assets. Investing in these is not unlike going short. However, there is an added advantage here: It's open to anyone. All you have to do is buy the funds. There is no need to borrow, and you do not have to have a margin account.

Here is how these short and leveraged ETFs get their exposure. Say you've got a long fund, like the ProShares Ultra Financials (UYG). What these do is help you double your returns with the Dow Jones US Financials Index, which means once the index rises, your returns will do the same.

Say the fund that would like to double the index currently has $500, then ProShares will have a whole basket of futures contracts, stocks, and swaps in that fund which will give it about %1000 in exposure, relative to that very index. So, your futures contracts as well as swaps are leveraged, and the stocks basket will allow you have exposure dollar for dollar.

Now let's take a look at a short fund, or a double short or triple short fund, which has the aim of giving you the index's exact opposite, two or three times of said opposite. Some really good examples would be the Direxion Daily Small Cap Bear 3x (TZA) and the UltraShort MSCI EAFE ProShares (EFU). The shorts work just like funds which go with double long positions, except that there is no going long, since these are clearly short funds.

Be aware of the risks that come with being leveraged, or going short. First of all, funds like this have crazy volatility. You can see really huge swings in price in a single day. They tend to go back and forth a lot, moving above then below the 200-period moving average. Volatility is good when you play it smart, and avoid getting burnt. Another thing you must recall is that there is no buying and holding here. You short, and you do so for the short term. As time progresses, you'll notice that they have the tendency of moving away from their benchmarks. While the funds will track according to their goals each day, the fact remains that given enough time, on account of the fact that they reset each new day, the performance on the whole will not really be the same as the indexes being shorted. So, keep the 200-day exponential moving average front and center as you trade these, and know that these trades will be happening quickly.

More Bank for Your Buck

There are lots of short and leveraged ETFs for you to play with, if you want to focus on major indexes, commodities, currencies, and sectors. Here's some of the funds you can play with:

- ProShares Ultra Consumer Services (UCC), which is two times the Dow Jones US Consumer Services Index average day's performance
- ProShares UltraShort S&P 500 (SDS), which is two times the inverse of the S&P 500 Index average day's performance.
- Rydex Inverse 2x S&P MidCap 400 (RMS), which is two times the inverse of the Mid Cap 400 Index average day's performance
- Rydex 2x S&P Select Sector Technology (RTG), which is two times the Technology Select Sector Index average day's performance
- Direxion Developed Markets Bull 3 Shares (DZK), which is three times the MSCI EAFE Index average day's performance
- Direxion Technology Bear 3x Shares (TYP), which is three times the inverse of the Russell 1000 Technology Index average day's performance

Criticisms of Short and Leveraged ETFs

A lot of the criticisms faced by these kinds of ETFs are

based on unfounded myths, so we'll tackle these right away.

First of all, there are those who believe that the problem with leveraged ETFs is that they are too easy to access, and as a result the average investor is in for a world of hurt. The fact is that there is nothing wrong with having options. More options are always a good thing. As long as the investor is aware of the inherent risks, there should not be a problem. Also, companies that give leveraged ETFs make it clear that these are not for just any investor, since they want their investors to succeed just as much as they want to succeed. Also, for the most part, it's mostly the bigger players who dabble in these.

Another myth is that these kinds of ETFs are simply to allow the investor to do away with margin issues. No, that is not the case. It simply makes it a lot easier for your average Joe or Jane to use a strategy hey couldn't before. Also, margin rules are in place mostly to keep banks sage, and not investors. The investor loses only what goes into their accounts, and nothing more.

There are those who believe the market goes down because of said leveraged funds. However, the blame is misplaced here. When it comes to the government doing their best to save the state of finance, it's just not an easy thing. Yes, there has been an increase in trading, as well as the interests that accrue, but the fact is that of the billions of trades made daily, leveraged ETFs only make up a handful and the blame they get is largely disproportionate. In fact, leveraged ETFs have proven themselves to be beneficial to the health of the market.

Some people do not like the fact that these are not investments that are friendly to buying and holding. The point of these is to allow you to hedge when the market goes against your long positions, and to allow you to make money even if the market is going the opposite direction. These are for hedging, and not for growing your retirement money.

Finally, there are those who say that leveraged ETFs are pointless because they do not work. Actually, they work fine, as they should. As time passes, you will notice that the returns are compounded. Where the market goes down, you get to make twice whatever you invested in going short using a leveraged ETF. You'd have to be blind to not see the benefit in that.

Conclusion

We've finally come to the very end of this book. The fact that you have read to this point says that you really do want to get into ETF investing, and that is great! You are ready to trade what you see, and not what you think, so that you can begin making a nice chunk of change. You know when to buy and when to sell, and you know not to get married to your trades.

Now, I need to make something extremely clear: Just because you read a book about something, does not automatically make you an expert. You're going to need lots and lots of practice, so you can get a real taste of what it's like to be in the markets. You have got to be disciplined, 100 percent. It would make no sense for you to go into this and only apply the strategy you have learned half the time, and the rest of the time you jump in and out of trades willy nilly. This is a fast and sure way to lose your money, and I hate to think you bought this book only to not practice what you were taught. You can make money with ETFs, but you have simply got to decide that you will commit yourself fully to this. Only then will you succeed.

There are several websites that will allow you to practice

the 200-exponential moving average strategy, so you can get a feel for it. If you want to jump right into trading with live funds, then you might want to start off with only a small percentage of the actual amount you would like to invest.

I want you to know that not all of your trades will be winners, and that's okay. However, as long as you make use of a stop loss, your winning trades will not just take care of the losses, but give you something to pocket and enjoy as well.

Keep in mind that this is something you can do on your own. You just need to be focused. You need to be determined, and unwilling to be distracted from your goals. There will be times when you break your trading strategy rules, especially in the beginning, it happens. Rather than keep trading, come back the next day, and begin anew when your emotions are balanced.

I personally have made the switch to ETFs, and I have not looked back. Once you know what you should know, you'll know why this is one of the best ways to invest, and you'll commit, too. This is the goal of writing this book: To convince you to get involved in the wonderful world of ETFs. I love how transparent things are, and I love the fact that I can diversify, I have options, and I am not buried in costs. These are more than enough reasons for you to get started with ETFs.

You might want to consider getting an advisor to help you along your ETF investing journey. Choose one who sees the same vision you do. You want an advisor who is always in touch with you, then you'd better get that kind. Figure out what you need in terms of communication. You need an advisor who will listen, and understand your concerns. The best kind of advisor does not care for pushing you into getting involved in products you're not interested in. They are more concerned with figuring out your needs and philosophy, and then giving you financial advice that is bespoke to you.

Before I wrap this up completely, I need to say something: Whatever you do, do not take on more risk than your portfolio can handle. There are those who do this, and invest it all in things that are incredibly volatile. There are also those who do not take on as much risk as they should, so that their money yields them next to nothing. If you want to make money, then you've got to be comfortable with taking risks. That said, you should never go overboard. Speak with your financial advisor, so that they can let you know how you should allocate your funds, and you don't wind up losing all your money.

Okay, that's pretty much it. Investing is a skill that you can hone over time, as you put in the work, and expose yourself to more and more knowledge about ETFs, as well as hands on practice. Do not allow yourself to feel intimidated. The more you practice, the better you get. It's just like riding a bike. Once you know how to ride one, you never really forget, do you? It simply becomes a part of you. Once your trading and investing become boring to you, then you will have definitely achieved mastery, as you no longer allow yourself to be swayed by the markets, and you control your risk properly, which will give you the very best in rewards, for sure.

REFERENCES

Appleby, Denise. "ETFs for Your 401(k)." Investopedia. www.forbes.com/personalfinance/retirementcollege/2007/07/25/etfs-401k-iras-pf-educationin_da_07 5investopedia_inl.html

Arnott, Rob. "Rob Arnott Discusses the Fundamental Approach to Stock Market Indexing: Pimco Bonds." www.pimco.com/leftnav/product+focus/2005/arnott+fundamental+indexing+interview.htm

Bailyn, Russell. "Indexes: What You Should Know." Russell Bailyn's Financial Planning Blog. www.russellbailyn.com/weblog/2007/04/indexes_what_you_should_know.html

Barker, Bill. "70 Times Better Than the Next Microsoft." The Motley Fool. www.fool.com/investing/small-cap/2006/01/12/70-times-better-than-thenext-microsoft.aspx

Culloton, Dan. "Sector ETFs: Use at Your Own Risk." Morningstar. http://news.morningstar.com/articlenet/article.aspx?id=166206&_qsbpa=y Culloton,

Dan. "A Surprise Entry in the Race for Actively Managed ETFs." Morningstar.

http://news.morningstar.com/articlenet/article.aspx?id=1933
50 &_QSBPA=Y&etfsection=Comm4&t1=1187276492
Custodio, Tony. "How Large Are Large-Cap Stocks?"
401Kafe.
www.infoplease.com/finance/tips/money/moneyman_101199.html

Dawson, Chester. "Emerging Markets: Beyond the Big Four." BusinessWeek.
www.businessweek.com/magazine/content/05_52/b3965450.htm Delfeld, Carl. "Are HealthShares ETFs Too Specialized?" Chartwell Advisor at Seeking Alpha. http://seekingalpha.com/article/35024-arehealthshares-etfs-too-specialized

Investopedia. "Exchange Traded Notes—An Alternative to ETFs." www.investopedia.com/articles/06/ETNvsETF.asp

Investopedia. "Introduction to Small Caps."
www.investopedia.com/articles/01/080101.asp

Investopedia. "Junk Bonds: Everything You Need to Know." www.investopedia.com/articles/02/052202.asp

Investopedia. "Margin Trading: What Is Buying on Margin?"
www.investopedia.com/university/margin/margin1.asp

Investopedia. "When Fear and Greed Take Over."
www.investopedia.com/articles/01/030701.asp
Investopedia. "Yield."
www.investopedia.com/terms/y/yield.asp Investorwords. "Definition of Collective Trust." www.investorwords.com/5462/collective_trust.html

McCall, Matthew. "Hedge against Corrections with Short ETFs." Investopedia.
http://research.investopedia.com/news/IA/2007/Hedge_Against_Corrections_With_Short_ETFs.aspx

McClatchy, Will. "Specialty Medical ETFs." ETFZone at Forbes.com. www.forbes.com/etfs/2007/04/05/xshares-healthshares-medical-pf-etfin_wm_0404soapbox_inl.html

Middleton, Timothy. "Buy the S&P 500 with Better Returns." MSN Money.
http://moneycentral.msn.com/content/p100259.asp

Wilcox, Cort. "Growth vs. Value: What's the Difference?" CDAPress.com.
www.postfallspress.com/articles/2007/07/08/business/bus03.txt

Wood, Carol A. "Real Estate Plays, Hassle-Free." BusinessWeek.
www.businessweek.com/investor/content/jul2005/pi20050721_3055_pi051.htm

Manufactured by Amazon.ca
Bolton, ON

Manufactured by Amazon.ca
Bolton, ON

37257441R00146